SETTLI
FRA**

A Household Guide and Cookery Book

i

Acknowledgements

To my American friend, Carol Robinson, who brilliantly summed up that weird out of place lostness that you experience when you uproot and move to France. As she said – "lost in Leclerc, confused in Carrefour, jinxed in Jardiland" - sums up the frustration when you want to make something, but don't know what it's called or where to find it.

Thanks also to Marie Lachèze for all her help in editing the contents and grammar and her support in this venture.

So too, thanks to Sue Hilliard for her practiced eye on format and style, and her idea for the French flag plate, which for my husband, Frank, translated into hours of photography, of plates, casserole dishes, tables, knives and forks, spades and forks, scones and so forth as we struggled to bring the disparate ideas of the book into one image.

Thanks to Jackie Johnstone for endless patience and for distilling all of Frank's photos to bring the cover design to life and then sorting out my interior photos, several times over, from colour to black and white, from low resolution to high, to fit in with the requirements of eBooks and print!

My thanks also to readers (especially Jane Widgery, Chris Busschers and Françoise Goater Cippola) who have made significant efforts to correct errors, and who have also contributed some great new tips.

Last, but not least, my daughter Gabby, who looked for consistency in my use of metric measures (and found none!).

Contents

How to use this Book.

This is not a book for reading from cover to cover, more something to be dipped into, a reference book if you like.

It has been designed to be small enough to pop into your bag when shopping. You can then look up the relevant section. For example, you may be shopping for fish. The fish section will then give you a subject-specific mini-dictionary listing fish names in English and French. Likewise, tools for your garden, or different types of flour and names of raising agents.

The font size is generous enough to make the book readable even when you've forgotten your reading glasses.

With a table of contents at the front and an index of all the recipes at the end of the book, it should be easy to find specific subjects quite quickly.

Preface

On my bookshelf here in France, I rediscovered an old book entitled 'Kenya Settler's Cookery Book and Household Guide' published in 1947 which prompted me to write this book along similar lines. After all, many of us find it hard enough when we come to live in France having to learn the language and deal with the bureaucracy, for instance, without wondering what puff pastry is called, or why *'praline'* is used for planting hedges as well as being a delicious confection of nuts and caramel.

This book does not cover the ground of many other books on buying and renovating a property in France, nor does it advise on legal matters such as inheritance or other taxes or even laws which can change every month, but attempts to fill the gap of ordinary life - shopping, everyday paperwork, gardening etc.

From shop to pot

To begin with, this book gives you the names for cooking ingredients in France and where to buy them. It answers questions such as 'what is baking powder called here?', and 'where can you buy double cream?' and includes an explanation of some weights and measures for those of us who live in France but rely ever more heavily on the internet for recipe inspiration.

From potager (vegetable plot) to pot

The second part of the book deals with what you might grow in your garden *'potager'*, and what to do with any produce so that you will have a collection of delicious recipes, designed to deal with any glut. This section contains a useful list of French gardening vocabulary and some tips for gardening in France - a place both warmer and colder than the UK.

Other things that might drive you potty

As well as the sections on buying and growing food, I have included some DIY tips such as buying firewood - sections on where to get information on the healthcare system and tips regarding paperwork in general. There are also sections on amusing tangles with the French language, the French postal system and organisations where you can get help; how to type accented letters on a PC QWERTY keyboard, useful books and useful apps and some tips on fitting in socially.

In the process of reading this book, you will also pick up quite a bit of French vocabulary.

FROM SHOP TO POT

What's it called?

Armed with a dictionary and access to huge supermarkets there shouldn't be a problem finding just what you need to make that dessert or cake that your family love. The problem is that even armed with a large copy of Larousse on your smart phone, it doesn't help when translations are sometimes just plain wrong, or difficult to find because you are trying to look up more than one word.

The most frequent amongst these is 'fresh cream'. For the French it's very easy – 'fresh cream' is 'crème fraîche' because they have no concept of what we mean by fresh cream. You will find many recipes online that fall into this trap. We even had a leaflet from our local *déchetterie* (waste/recycling plant) which gave a wonderful recipe in three languages – French, English and Dutch – which explained what to do with 'withered' lettuce rather than throw it out. Whichever language version you had followed, the result would have been different because the English version used 'fresh cream' and the French version used 'crème fraîche'. The choice of adjective would have put off many English readers who are used to the idea of eating greens that have been wilted in a pan but 'withered? – now that conjures up a whole different picture, of something dry and wrinkled from age or disease.

One thing to look out for when shopping in France is the 'red label'. The Red Label is not a brand, but an official sign of superior quality.

When buying cheese look for AOC, a French guarantee of quality recognized worldwide. AOC *'Appellation d'Origine Contrôlée'* is the denomination of a region or a locality, used to designate a product of the region which has quality and characteristics that are exclusively or essentially derived from the geographic environment. A similar label AOP *'Appellation d'Origine Protégée'* as well as assuring a product's geographic provenance, guarantees impeccable quality. These appellations are used for other products as well, such as wine, butter, lentils and lavender.

Dairy products

- Cream
- Milk
- Butter
- Yogurt & Desserts
- Cheese

Cream

Until very recently, cream has been one of those products you got friends to bring back from the UK as it was impossible to buy it in a form that we recognise. The French tend to put *'crème pâtissière'* (thick custard) in cakes rather than whipped cream. No fresh cream apple turnovers here - the nearest thing is a *'chausson au pomme'*, an apple turnover without cream and an éclair is filled not with fresh cream but with *'crème pâtissière'* flavoured with chocolate or coffee.

Years ago, in the UK you could buy single cream and double cream, as well as sour cream and crème fraîche. Over the years that has been extended to include whipping cream (somewhere between single and double cream), and then various thickened creams (usually with carrageenan). In France, until very recently it was virtually impossible to buy what we call 'fresh cream'. If you asked for fresh cream, you got crème fraîche.

There is no English translation for crème fraîche; it is uniquely French and so crème fraîche it remains in English (and Dutch), perhaps without the accent! Crème fraîche has a creamy texture and while it is not at all like sour cream or yoghurt neither is it a sweet cream. Crème fraîche, sour cream, and yogurt all use special bacteria to give them their taste but crème fraîche does not have the tang of sour cream or yogurt. To cooked dishes, crème fraîche adds a unique taste and does not curdle like sour cream.

When cream is not pasteurized or sterilized, the word 'crue' (raw) is then mandatory on the labelling, with a sweet flavour and a very short shelf life which is probably why it is very so hard to find. Virtually all the cream you can buy is heat-treated (pasteurisation, simple sterilisation or Ultra High Temperature sterilisation - UHT) which lengthens its life and helps prevent the spread of TB.

There are thickened 'épais' versions of the liquid types of cream. The thickening agent is usually carrageenan (derived from seaweed.) These do not hold well and are perhaps better reserved for serving with fruit rather than decorating cakes.

What cream then is best to use to make whipped cream that will hold?

*The percentage of **fat**, 'matières grasses'(mg) affects how well cream will whip, and how long it will hold.*

If you want to achieve something like a thick whipped double/heavy cream, mix mascarpone cheese with 'Crème Fleurette de Normandie Entière'.

Recently a commercial version of this mixture has appeared in some supermarkets. It is also possible to buy 1 litre packs of cream 35%mg, which will hold well whilst chilled. It usually has a label suggesting it is for professional use – e.g. 'Crème pour Professionnel', or 'PRO' as shown in the photo.

Supermarkets also sell small packets called 'Chantifix', which is used to help thicken whipped cream. It contains sugar, modified starch, gelling agent (carrageenan) and aroma.

UK/US definitions		French Equivalent
Single cream	23% fat - General purpose cooking cream suitable for pouring over desserts and using in coffee	Crème légère 12 – 21% mg.
Light Cream	18-30% -Roughly equivalent to UK single cream	Crème légère 12 – 21% mg.
Double cream	**48% fat** -Whips easily and can be used for piping	Not available
Heavy cream (US)	36% + - Can be whipped but not as thick as UK double cream	Crème pour Professionnel 35%mg
Whipping cream	35% fat - Can be whipped but less thick than double cream and may not pipe very well	Crème Liquide Entière[1] de Normandie - 30% mg
Clotted cream	55% fat -Specialised cream comes from Devon and Cornwall. It can be made slowly in your oven overnight – 12 hours at 80C. Chill for a further 10 hours. Don't use UHT cream.	Not available

---

[1] Depending on the brand, the cream has added ingredients. For example, **Elle & Vire** is cream and a thickener (carrageenan), and **Envia** is cream, emulsifants: (pork gélatine) and two thickeners: xanthan gum, carrageenan. The latter brand to be avoided by several religious groups as well as vegetarians and vegans.

UK/US definitions		French Equivalent
Sour/ed cream	18% fat -soured and thickened by the controlled action of lactic acid bacteria	Not available
Crème fraîche	15-30% - Another soured cream (but not cream that has gone off - and not fresh cream!)	Crème fraîche
Custard	Easy to buy. It is light pouring custard, made with sugar, egg yolks and milk, usually flavoured with vanilla - not the yellow powder used to make custard in the UK.	Crème anglaise
Pastry cream sometimes called crème pat.	This is a rich, creamy custard thickened with flour. It is a key ingredient of many French desserts such as soufflés, fruit tarts and mille-feuille. It is much thicker than crème anglaise.	Crème pâtissière

Milk

I'm told that supermarkets carry fresh milk mainly for foreigners. If the locals buy milk, they buy UHT. Although the cut-price supermarkets are yet to stock it, the bigger supermarkets certainly stock the following:

English	French	Bottle
Whole milk	Lait entier	Red top
Semi-skimmed milk	Lait demi-écrémé	Blue top
Skimmed milk	Lait écrémé	Green top
Cultured Buttermilk	Lait fermenté / lait ribot	With Arabic writing on the side
Unpasteurised milk	Lait cru	Yellow top
Condensed Milk/	Lait concentré sucré	Cans or tubes
Evaporated milk	Lait concentré non-sucré	As above

Most of these items will be found in the chiller cabinets, but the condensed milk *'lait concentré sucre'* and evaporated milk *'Lait concentré non-sucré'* do not need to be chilled and will be found with all the other long-life and powdered milk products.

Butter

Most of the butter sold is unsalted '*doux*', and so goes off rather quickly. Lightly salted butter '*demi-sel*' is available, and an 'easy-to-spread' version '*beurre tendre*²' is also available. A recent addition to the shelves is reduced fat butter '*beurre à teneur réduite en matière grasse*', which varies but is typically 60% of the fat of normal butter, no reduction of price for the added water! Quite a few of the more expensive kinds of butter have added salt crystals, and some are churned in the old-fashioned way. There are '*bio*' versions of butter too, known as 'organic' in the UK.

Another butter I've seen in the supermarkets recently is "*spécial cuisson*", or cooking butter, which has been clarified to remove the particles that burn at higher temperatures. It has an even higher fat percentage than normal butter and is ideal for making flaky pastry, for example. It has 899 kcals for 100 grams compared to 753 kcals for normal butter, and 547 kcals for 60% reduced fat butter.

---

²Soft butter is made by modifying its chemical composition. Butter is a mixture of fatty acids (82%), milk proteins and water (16%). Fatty acids are of two types: saturated or unsaturated, the latter melting at a higher temperature than the former. The agri-food manufacturers therefore maintain the butter at a temperature of about 20° and recover the liquid fraction which is mainly composed of saturated fatty acids. This fraction is added to whole butter. The resulting mixture thus acquires a lower melting temperature than normal butter and remains soft even in the refrigerator.

Yogurt and desserts

The supermarkets have chiller cabinets full of various kinds of yogurt *'yaourt'* and dairy desserts, as well as shelves full of non-dairy desserts, mostly for children. The latter are very popular in hospitals too.

Cheese

France has always been known for its vast array of cheeses, in fact, there is a famous quote from Générale de Gaulle *"How can you govern a country that has two hundred and forty-six varieties of cheese?"* These days the UK has caught up. The British Cheese Board states that 'there are over 700 named British cheeses produced in the UK' and I'm sure there are probably more than 1000 French cheeses now. If you want to buy English cheeses in France, then the big supermarkets often carry cheddar, especially in the tourist season, but often it is the vacuum-packed plastic kind. Stilton is a rarity, but Shropshire Blue is nearly always available in Grand Frais. The bigger supermarkets carry enormous stocks of cheese and specialist cheese shops – *fromageries* - carry even more varieties, even lesser-known British cheeses.

When buying French cheese, it is perhaps helpful to look out for quality which is indicated by the AOP/AOC labelling standard. There are three families of cheese to choose from; when making up a cheeseboard for dinner it is a good idea to choose at least one from each family.

Pressed Cheeses

The first group of cheeses are pressed cheeses all of which are made from cow's milk, *'fromage de vache'*, including:

Cantal

Cantal is the cheese that is the closest to English cheddar, although it has a somewhat different taste. It is a pressed, uncooked cow's milk cheese from the Auvergne mountains and is one of the oldest cheeses in history. It can weigh between 35 and 45 kg and is aged for a minimum of 30 days to more than 6 months for an old Cantal. Two other varieties produced nearby are Salers and Laguiole. Made from the milk of cows grazing at high altitude.

Comté

This is from the Franche Comté region of eastern France. The production area stretches along the Swiss border, and all milk comes from cows grazing at an altitude of at least 400 metres. Comté is the traditional cheese used in a cheese "*fondue*", and for "*raclette*"

Cheeses like Comté include Beaufort and Abondance which are made in a similar manner in the French Alps. Beaufort tends to be stronger tasting than Comté, and the taste is also slightly different.

Gruyère

This is a pressed cooked cheese often sold grated '*râpé*. Traditional on toast floated on French onion soup.

Emmental

Emmental is a traditional cheese with holes in it. Often found grated '*râpé*' in supermarkets.

Mimolette

A round cheese made in the area of Lille in the north of France. Its orange colour is the result of the addition of natural colouring. It comes in young and old '*vieille*' versions.

Reblochon

Another ancient cheese, Reblochon has been in existence since the Middle Ages. It is a rich soft pressed cheese made in the Savoie region; it has quite a strong flavour, and a creamy texture. It is traditionally used in '*Tartiflette*', which is made with potatoes, Reblochon cheese, lardons and onions.

Soft Cheeses

The second family of cheeses encompasses literally hundreds of soft cheeses; each region has its own specialities. Many of these - notably those with *appellation contrôlée* - are manufactured in small units, and usually, you buy a whole cheese, except for Brie and St. Nectaire.

Brie

Brie is the ancestor of all soft cheeses. There are two sorts of Brie, Brie de Meaux and Brie de Melun, both *appellation contrôlée* (AOC) cheeses named after two nearby towns in the country some fifty miles south east of Paris. Brie comes as a thin round cheese about 20 inches in diameter, with a soft white crust. This crust is eaten, not cut off

Camembert:

A cheese from Normandy, a ripe Camembert should be just soft on the inside, but not too runny. A young Camembert will tend to be hard and dry, and rather tasteless; an overripe Camembert, going yellowish on the outside, will tend to smell quite strongly. The crust of a Camembert is usually eaten.

Mont d'Or

This very distinctive *appellation contrôlée* cheese from Franche Comté is manufactured along the French-Swiss border, at altitudes of at an altitude of least 800 metres. It is a rind washed cheese matured in a round frame made of a thin strip of local spruce wood which imparts a delicious aroma to the cheese. Unfortunately, Mont d'Or is a seasonal cheese and is only made between August 15 and March 15. It is one of the few kinds of cheese that can be eaten with a spoon as it is so runny. This cheese comes with an undulating beige crust, and under the crust the cheese itself is soft. Mont d'Or is very tasty heated in the oven, until runny, with a clove of garlic and a tablespoon of white wine and dipped with chunks of French bread. This can be done with a good Camembert.

Pont l'Évêque

A creamy soft cheese, uncooked and unpressed, from the coastal region of Normandy, south of Deauville; this is one of the oldest cheeses in France and has been documented since the 12th century.

Blue Cheeses

Blue cheeses comprise the third family of cheeses.

Bleu d'Auvergne

Bleu d'Auvergne is a cow's milk blue-veined AOC cheese whose quality and taste can vary considerably, going from the bland to the sharp.

Saint Agur,

A creamy blue cheese made in the Velay hills of Haute Loire.

Bleu de Bresse

Bleu de Bresse is a commercially made blue cheese that was first made in the Bresse area of France in the 1950s. It was developed in response to the growing popularity of Italian cheeses.

Bleu des Causses (AOC)

Is generally delicious and strong tasting, without being sharp. A cows-milk cheese, sometimes quite crumbly, manufactured in the same area as Roquefort and quite similar tasting, but less salty.

Fourme d'Ambert

A mild blue cheese from the Auvergne, often with an almost nutty flavour.

Roquefort

The most famous French blue cheese made from the milk of the "Lacaune" breed of sheep. The cheese has been made since the Middle Ages and has been famous for many centuries. It is made in the *'causses'* mountains of southern France, in the department of the Aveyron, and matured in caves.

There are, of course, many other kinds of cheese, for example:

Goat's cheeses:

Goats cheese is available in many forms and is known as *'fromage de chèvre'*. Examples include *'cabécou'*, Crottin de Chavignol, Valençay, etc. Many local producers market their cheese under their own local village or regional name. Goats' cheeses can be sold either very young *'frais'* when they are soft and spreadable'; medium matured, when they are still soft, but not spreadable; or fully matured, when they are hard.

Ewe's milk cheeses:

Like Roquefort which is made with ewe's milk 'Ossau-Iraty' is a pressed, uncooked ewe's milk cheese - *'fromage de brebis'*. It is a product of the Pays-Basque and Bearn regions.

Raclette:

'Raclette', is a meal in which thin slices of Comté or even Cantal cheese are heated and melted then poured over baked potatoes and eaten with gherkins, *'jambon'* and other accompaniments. It is an easy and convivial meal, where everyone helps themselves from the raclette grill which is placed in the middle of the table. However, you can buy "raclette" cheese, but this is a mass-produced industrial cheese.

Generic terms:

The words *'tomme'* and *'fourme'* are generic words that can describe several different types of French cheese. The French word for cheese, *'fromage'* is a diminutive of the word *'fourme'*.

There is no doubt that the French are immensely proud of their cheeses and treat them with a great deal of reverence. There is an etiquette as to how cheese is cut, as illustrated by this diagram from a supermarket. The correct way to eat cheese is to start with the mild

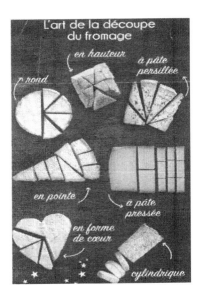

flavoured ones before going onto the smellier and blue cheeses which will take over your taste buds. In France, cheese is served before dessert, and with a knife and fork or some bread – never crackers. It is customary always to serve a choice of at least 3 cheeses and not to help yourself to more than 3 different varieties.

Note, in France the bread is always put directly on the table next to your plate – not lodged on the edge of your plate.

The other thing to note is that French people do not bite lumps off things – you break off a piece of bread and pop that into your mouth. You cut a piece off an apple and pop that in your mouth. Wherever possible you use a knife and fork, rather than your hands.

Mini-Dictionary – Dairy Products

English	French
Pouring custard	Crème anglaise
Thick custard	Crème pâtissière
Creme fraiche (not fresh cream)	Crème fraîche
Percentage fat – (*whip ability*)	Mg or Matières grasses
Whole cream / light cream liquid	Crème entière / légère
Raw - unprocessed	Cru(e)
Cream from Normandy - pasteurised	Crème de lait de Normandie
Thickened cream	Crème épaisse
A product that thickens cream	Chantifix
Cream/shop selling dairy products	Crème / Crémerie (or crèmerie)
Skimmed / Semi-skimmed	Ecrémé / Demi-écrémé
Butter milk (Arabic on pack)	Lait fermenté / lait Ribot
Condensed milk / evaporated milk	Lait concentré sucré/non-sucré
Unsalted butter	Beurre doux
Semi-salted butter	Beurre demi-sel
Butter spreadable from the fridge	Beurre tendre
Reduced fat butter	Beurre à teneur réduite en mg
Cheese / shop selling cheese	Fromage / fromagerie
Sheep	Brebis
Goat	Chèvre
Cow	Vache

Baking Goods

- Flour
- Raising Agents
- Sugar
- Oils & Fats
- Spices
- Pastry
- Dried Fruits
- Nuts

Flour

In the UK (as a gross over-simplification), we usually have the choice of plain flour used for things like Yorkshire pudding, or self-raising (rising) flour, used for cakes, or strong flour for making bread (white, brown, and some specials). Of course, there is also a range of flours made from grains other than wheat, such as rice flour and cornflour (corn starch) for making sauces.

English	French
Wheat flour	Farine de blé
Wheat bran	Son de blé
Self-raising flour	Farine à gâteaux avec poudre levante
Spelt	Épeautre
Barley – Pearl barley	Orge – Orge perlé
Rye	Seigle
Oats	Avoine
Oat Bran	Son d'avoine
Oat flakes/rolled oats	Flocons d'avoine
Chestnut flour	Farine de châtaigne
Cornflour/corn-starch	Farine de maïs (Maizena)

Grades of flour

In France wheat 'le blé' and rye 'le seigle' flours are subject to classification by type. What is this? It is not generally something we have to concern in the UK unless it is Italian 'Type 00' flour used for pasta.

The 'type' of flour defines the degree of milling, the lower the number, the less the flour contains remnants of bran or husk. The browner the flour, the more husk it contains, which means a greater likelihood of herbicides, insecticides etc being found in the flour, unless you choose organic[3] i.e. *'bio'* flour.

In the UK we look for flour designated as 'strong' which distinguishes flour with a relatively high level of gluten which is required to provide enough elasticity in the dough to contain the air when the yeast rises. Apparently, in France, the higher the type number the 'stronger' the flour. However, some kinds of wheat are harder (stronger) than others, so this does not necessarily follow, but the table below is a rough guide.

---

[3]In January 2019, the French consumer magazine '60 Millions de consommateurs', tested 65 products sold in boulangeries and supermarkets in France and found that more than half contain controversial substances such as additives, pesticides and mycotoxins and some included endocrine disruptors, and immune effects in humans. They also said there was too much salt in all the products tested, and especially in baguettes.

Flour types

	UK	France	USA
Milled from 100% of the whole grain	Wholemeal Flour	Farine Intégrale 150	Whole-wheat flour
Some of the bran removed leaving about 85% of the grain	Brown flour	Farine complète Type 110	First clear flour
White Bread Flour	Strong bread flour	80	High gluten bread flour
White Bread Flour		65	
White flour	Plain flour	Tous usages type 55	All-purpose flour
Very fine flour from the early stages of roller milling	Patent flour	Farine Fluide Type 45	Pastry flour

As I mentioned the flours from different countries are not directly comparable, so you will need to experiment. Very strong flour which is used for baking bread in the UK is not easily available in France. If like me, you enjoy a proper wholemeal loaf then it is worth importing some 'very strong wholemeal' flour. But be warned, twice I've been stopped at the airport, for an inconveniently long time, to have my kilo of flour examined, as apparently, it looks like a liquid in the scanner – liquid in a paper bag?

Farine fluide is guaranteed not to go lumpy (*Garantie anti-grumeaux*) and is used for pancake batter, sauces, waffles, doughnuts and *crème pâtissière*. It is a 'type 45' flour.

'All-purpose' i.e. *tous usages* is Type 55, is slightly less fine than *farine fluide* and is used for everyday French bread.

Flour for making cakes, like the UK 'self-raising (rising) flour' – '*Farine à gâteaux avec poudre levante*' - is also available in the supermarkets. You may see it as '*Farine de Blé pour gâteau, poudre à lever incorporée*'. Of course, you can use chemical raising agents from a small packet with plain flour – see *Levure Chimique* or just add bicarbonate of soda. It's not unusual to hear expat cake makers saying they need to add baking powder to the local self-raising flour, so you will need to experiment.

Flour mixes

There is a big choice of flour in the supermarkets, and some of it comes with yeast already incorporated for making bread '*pain*', or pizza, or brioche etc. Personally, if I'm not buying and eating a lovely crusty baguette from a boulangerie, then I really love a good stone ground wholemeal loaf. Much as I like crusty French bread, it needs to be bought at least once a day as it goes stale so quickly, which means you can end up wasting a lot, even if you do make baguette dumplings[4]. We haven't taken to the sliced white bread in our local supermarkets as most of it is too sweet for British tastes.

---

[4] See Rachel Khoo's Boeuf bourguignon with baguette dumplings

Making Bread

Having made many very good loaves in my bread machine, I started getting the odd loaf that was as flat as a dab. At first, I thought maybe I had a packet of yeast which had gone bad. But then I got a whole spate of barely edible flat loaves and after some experimentation, I found out why some books tell you to make bread with bottled water. Even though we have 4 filters on our water before it comes into the kitchen, one of them being for chlorine, there are days when you can still smell

the chlorine, and we concluded it was on those days that the bread came out flat.

Since then I always use bottled water (any kind) when making bread as it is less likely to contain chlorine or other chemicals that might affect the yeast. I've not had a flat loaf since.

Making Pizza

One of the outbuildings on our property is a large bread oven, '*four au pain*'. It's a bit puzzling why there should be such a large stand-alone bread oven in our grounds which are not close to anyone else -

the bread-oven being at least 50 meters from the house, which in its former days was little more than a one-room farmhouse with a barn attached.

We felt that to light it just to make one loaf would be an enormous effort and waste of wood. We knew nothing about using a wood-fired bread oven, although our predecessors had left us a nice pile of bundled dry twigs tied up with wire. As is often the case, the internet came to our rescue and informed us that the oven would be hot enough to bake bread or pizza when the roof of the oven turned white.

Then we visited a pizza 'club' nearby, and from them learnt how to make pizza dough. Next, we decided to get to know our neighbours and have a pizza party, and of course, on the day we chose to do this, it poured with rain. They blamed us for bringing English weather with us, but luckily the bread-oven building was big enough for us to all huddle inside.

When we have a pizza party some folk bring bread and pastries to bake in the oven alongside the pizza.

What we learnt from the pizza club, was the type of flour to use for making pizza. Recipes for pizza dough, or for making pasta, call for 'Type oo' flour (Italian grade easily found in UK supermarkets), which is approximately the equivalent to the French type 45, it's not a designation for a 'strong' flour (one with a lot of gluten). Puzzlingly, many recipes call for 'strong flour' when making pizza dough, but we found we were getting rather hard bases and subsequently found that type 45, or *farine fluide* is softer and much better, unless, perhaps, you are making a very thin pizza crust.

Raising agents

English	French	Description
Yeast	Levure Boulanger	Dried fast acting yeast in small packets is usually found close to the flour in supermarkets.
Bicarbonate of soda	Bicarbonate de soude	Also known as Bicarbonate *alimentaire*.
Cream of tartar	Crème de tartre	Also known as monopotassium tartrate.
Baking Powder	Levure Chimique, or poudre à lever	Maize starch with sodium bicarbonate and monopotassium tartrate.
Fresh Yeast	Levure fraîche	Small cubic packets in the supermarket chiller.

Sugar

Granulated Sugar (white)

Granulated sugar does not seem to be available in France. Their general-purpose sugar for baking etc. is more like the UK caster sugar. Their large grain sugar 'Sucre Cristal' is used for jam making.

Caster Sugar – or Superfine Sugar

'*Le sucre en poudre*', is like caster sugar. This is confusing for some of us, as you automatically think of icing sugar as powdered sugar, but that is known as '*Sucre Glacé*'

Icing Sugar – powdered sugar

Sucre Glacé is used for sprinkling onto cakes or for making royal icing. Known as powdered or 'confectioners' sugar' in America. Up to 3% corn-starch is added to keep it free flowing in the USA. (In France, silica is used.)

Nib sugar /pearl sugar

'*Sucre en grains*', hard to find in the UK, is used for baking in France and does not melt at temperatures typically used for baking. It is often used on '*chouquettes*', '*Tropéziennes*' and sometimes on '*Pains aux raisins*'

Jam making sugar

'*Sucre Cristal*' is the traditional sugar to make your homemade jams. The sugar grain of the Cristal is bigger than that of the powdered sugar and so melts more slowly and gives you a clearer jam.

'Gros Cristaux de sucre' has even larger grains of sugar which melt more slowly, and this helps preserve the flavour of the fruit.

'Confisuc' or *'Les Spéciaux Confitures et Gelées'*, are sugars with added pectin to allow you to make jams and jellies which will set in 5 minutes from fruits which are low in pectin, such as strawberries. Very often these are specific to the fruit you are going to use – for example, apricots or strawberries. There is even one, *'Confitures Allégées'*, which for making jam with 30% less sugar than normal.

In the absence of these specialised sugars, you can also add pectin yourself using 'Vitpris' (see photo).

Brown sugar

You will see brown sugar called 'Blonvilliers' that is obtained from sugar cane which is lighter than another brown sugar called '*cassonade*' also obtained from sugar cane. You will also see '*Sucre la Perruche*', again a cane sugar, a bit darker than 'Blondvilliers'. Soft dark brown sugar or muscovado (i.e. raw sugar) is known as '*sucre complet moscovade*' and is generally only found in '*bio*' shelves. This may be found with dried fruits rather than the other sugars usually found next to the flour.

Note: The French do not tend to use bowls of loose sugar. They prefer sugar lumps '*petits morceaux*', or these days sometimes little paper packets of sugar as you see in the cafés.

There are so many varieties of sugar available in France that it is worth going to one of the websites of some of the French suppliers – e.g.:

https://www.beghin-say.fr/sucres/tous-nos-sucres or

http://www.saintlouis-sucre.com/en/consumers/consumer-products/

Sugar facts:

France is the world's biggest producer of beet sugar, especially in the north. This is because Napoleon ordered that 28,000 hectares (69,000 acres) be devoted to growing the sugar beet in response to British blockades of cane sugar during the Napoleonic Wars, which ultimately stimulated the rapid growth of a European sugar beet industry. By 1840, about 5% of the world's sugar was derived from sugar beets, and by 1880, this number had risen to over 50%.

Interestingly, sugar can be used to slow down the setting of concrete. According to Richard Gray, Science correspondent of the Telegraph, in 2014 engineers working on London Underground's Victoria Line used sugar to help remove concrete that was accidentally poured over signalling equipment during upgrade work at Victoria Station. Depending on the kind of cement being used, even small amounts of sugar can double the time it takes to set.

Vitpris and pectin

Vitpris from Alsa is a gelling agent for making jams and jellies basically made from apple pectin. Whether to add pectin to jams and jellies depends on your taste buds, the level of pectin in your fruit and whether the appearance of the result is important to you. It reduces the time you need to get a set, and hence a brighter clearer result, but you can tell there is apple in the background. Adding a lemon or two often helps with the setting.

Oils and cooking fats

There is a large range of cooking oils in most supermarkets, some are good for frying and high temperature cooking, others better for drizzling or making salad-dressings. The table below indicates the French name for some of the many of the oils available. Of course, there are organic 'bio' versions of most, as well as extra virgin or refined. The lower temperature in the "smoking point[5]" column indicates the "extra virgin" version, where the higher temperature indicates the refined version of an oil, which breaks down at a higher temperature.

Cooking oil / fat	French	Smoking point
Peanut oil	Huile d'arachide	180C - 227C
Sunflower oil	Huile de tournesol	180C – 227C
Rapeseed oil	Huile de Colza	204C
Corn oil	Huile de maïs	180C - 227C
Coconut oil	Huile de noix de coco	177C - 232C
Olive oil	Huile d'olive	199C - 205C
Lard	Saindoux	188C
Butter	Beurre	120 - 150C
Ghee	Beurre clarifié	252C

---

[5] As you probably know, using oils or fats above their smoking point does more than impart a burnt flavour to foods. Overheating also creates harmful free radicals destroying beneficial nutrients and phytochemicals found in many unrefined oils.

Cooking oil / fat	French	Smoking point
Duck fat	Graisse de canard	190C
Grape seed oil	Huile de Pépins de Raisin	180C – 216C
Hazelnut oil	Huile de noisette	221C
Walnut oil	Huile de noix	160C – 204C
Sesame oil	Huile de sésame	177C – 210C

Walnuts being pressed for Oil

Spices

Most herbs and spices can be found in the supermarkets and in Asian supermarkets in the bigger towns but finding one or two are particularly troublesome to find.

Allspice

It is not unusual for folk to believe Allspice is a mixture of other spices, however, Allspice berries are hard black or brown dried berries about the size of a small pea. Allspice is sometimes labelled as Jamaican pepper – *'le poivre de Jamaïque'* or *'piment de la Jamaïque'*.

Quatre Épices

'Quatre Épices' is a mixture of ginger, cinnamon, clove and nutmeg. Used in the popular *'Pain d'épice'*.

Mixed Spice

Mixed spice is a purely British concoction, something for you to import as it is impossible to find in France. It is an aromatic blend of cinnamon, coriander, caraway, nutmeg, ginger and cloves, for adding to fruit cakes, puddings, gingerbread, hot cross buns and even some savoury dishes.

Cumin and caraway

These two seeds are so often confused in France / French translation and yet they are so different – different in flavour, from different climates, used in different types of cooking.

Cumin *'cumin'*, from a hot climate is cultivated primarily in India, and used in many curries and North African dishes. Caraway *'carvi'*, from a cold climate, grows in Europe and is used in many cakes, sauerkraut, schnapps, aquavit, and cheese. Unfortunately, if you look up 'cumin' in a dictionary, it will often be translated as '*carvi*'

Poppy Seeds – '*grains de pavot*'

These are the blue poppy seeds used in European pastry making, not the white poppy seeds used in many Indian dishes. The former are easy to find in France, the latter are not.

Pastry

Puff or flaky pastry – *'pâte feuilletée'*

In the UK it is possible to buy puff pastry ready to roll out, and you can end up with a nice thick flaky pastry top for a pie or use it to make sausage rolls for example. Here in France, you will find a somewhat different product – *'pâte feuilletée'* ready rolled. You can get a version made with pure butter. The result is much thinner than British puff pastry - but it is flaky and brilliant for making quiches and tarts and comes ready rolled in grease-proof paper, which saves on the washing up!

Whilst this can be found in most supermarkets; rectangular shapes seem to be available only in very large supermarkets or upmarket frozen food stores like Picard.

As with many of these things, you get what you pay for, so beware the cheaper versions.

Shortcrust pastry - *pâte brisée* and *pâte sablée*

Roughly equivalent to shortcrust pasty, you can also buy *pâte brisée* and *pâte sablée*. They are not as short, and *pâte sablée* is obviously the sweetened version. These also come pre-rolled and are in greaseproof paper, ready to line your tart tin.

Filo pastry and *Feuilles de brick*

Another kind of pastry you can buy in France is called Brick - *feuilles de brick*. This originates from North Africa is very thin and rather like filo which originates in Greece. They are not quite the same, with brick being slightly less fragile than filo, although plenty of expats use 'brick' in place of filo. Brick is good for making samosas, even if it is very different from the original skins made with atta[6] flour and folded differently - instructions are on the back of the packet. Brick comes ready-rolled in rounds with sheets of parchment paper in-between. Filo is also available in larger supermarkets.

Crumpets

Not known here, but the British product shelves in large supermarkets have been known to stock them occasionally.

---

[6]Wholemeal wheat flour, originating from the Indian subcontinent, has a high gluten content, which provides elasticity, so doughs made from atta flour are strong and can be rolled out into thin sheets, used for chapati and other flatbreads.

Dried Fruit

Dried fruit, candied peel, glace cherries, dried cranberries can all be found either with the cake-making ingredients, but usually in smallish quantities and very expensive.

In the UK we sometimes buy 'mixed dried fruit', if we want to make Christmas cake or Christmas pudding for example, but sometimes we may want to purchase currants, or sultanas or raisins separately and each has its own qualities. The problem here in France is to find out what they are called and where you can get them.

They are all sweet dried fruits that stem from different varieties of vine-grown grapes, all of which, in French, are known as 'raisin sec'. This is confusing if you are looking for what is known as a 'raisin' in the UK, whilst it is, in fact, a 'raisin sec' for us it is a specific product and not any old dried grape.

Raisins

Raisins are dried white Muscatel grapes. They are dried, normally in the sun, resulting in a dark, dried fruit like a currant, dense in texture yet bursting with a sweet flavour. A raisin can (unlike currants) soak up other flavours, which is why it is popular to soak raisins in flavoured alcohols such as brandy before using in cooking.

Sultanas

Sultanas are golden in colour and tend to be much plumper, sweeter, and juicier than other raisins. Also known as golden raisins, sultanas go through a different processing method, as well as a sulphur dioxide treatment, that gives these raisins their rich, golden hue.

Currants

Do not confuse soft fruit currants such as blackcurrants with the currants talked about here which are a dried grape. These currants are the dark, black currants you will find in Spotted Dick or an Eccles cake and they are, in fact, dried, dark red, seedless grapes, often the Black Corinth grape. The grapes are dried to produce a black, tiny, shrivelled, sweet flavour-packed fruit. The grapes were originally cultivated in the south of Greece and most often from the island of Zante, hence the name Zante Currant in the US. The name currant comes from the ancient city of 'Corinth', but in the UK and Ireland, they are simply called currants.

So, what we call raisins in the UK are not available here, what you will find are *'raisins secs or raisins blonds or sultanines'* – i.e. sultanas, or *'Raisins de Corinthe'* – i.e. currants.

When I first came here, I made some jelly from the excess grapes in our garden and wondered what to label it as in French, so I asked a group of French friends what they would call it. Obviously not grape jelly (jelly in the English, not American sense). I never did find out because they all said they had never come across it. I suppose that grapes are all reserved for wine making here – who would think of making *'confiture'* with grapes?

Here is some terminology, which might help in this minefield.

- *'Le raisin'* – fresh grape.
- *'Les raisins secs'* – dried grapes
- *'Une grappe de raisin'* – a bunch of grapes

Note the difference between 'grape' and *'grappe'*

Mincemeat

Mincemeat (usually Robertson's) is available here in some big supermarkets which have a 'British' section but at a price. Many people make their own, but that isn't cheap because the cost of the dried fruit is so high. Something worth bringing back with you.

Nuts

The dictionary translation for 'nut' is *'noix'*, but in France *'noix'* means WALNUT, not just any nut. Of course, there are almonds *'amandes'*, hazelnuts *'noisettes'*, sweet chestnuts *'châtaignes'*, cashew nuts *'noix de cajou'*, coconuts *'noix de coco'* and macadamia nuts, not to mention peanuts (*cacahouètes*), which of course are not nuts at all

but legumes.

Baking Goods Mini-Dictionary

English	French
Wholemeal flour	Farine complet - type 110
Flour with even more of the grain	Farine très complète – type 150
Lightest smoothest flour	Farine fluide – type 45
General purpose flour – used for baguettes	Farine tous usages – type 55
Cake flour with raising agent	Farine à gâteaux avec poudre levante
As above – self-raising / rising flour	Farine de Blé pour gâteau, poudre à lever incorporée
Bread oven	Four au pain
Flaky pastry	Pâte feuilletée
Short crust pastry but not short	Pâte brisée
As above with sugar	Pâte sucrée
Caster Sugar / bar sugar	Sucre en poudre
Icing sugar	Sucre glace
Sugar lumps – brown and white	Sucre en morceaux
Granulated sugar used for jam.	Sucre cristal
Pearl or nib sugar	Sucre en grains
Dark brown muscovado sugar	Sucre complet moscovade

English	French
Very thin pastry from North Africa	Feuilles de brick
From Greece and Turkey	Filo
Walnut	Noix
Almond	Amande
Hazelnut	Noisette
Sweet Chestnut	Châtaigne
American sweet chestnut used for making Marron Glacé	Marron
Cashew	Noix de cajou
Coconut	Noix de coco
Brazil Nut	Noix du Brésil
Peanuts	Cacahuètes (arachides)
Pine nuts	Pignons de pin

Drinks, Cereals, Biscuits

I've combined these three product types as they are very much aimed at children here.

There are no 'squashes' as in the UK, instead the French have fruit *sirops*, which are very good and used in a similar way. *Sirops* are also available in sugar free

Breakfast cereals are largely aimed at children and not eaten by adults. The vast majority are chocolate based. The supermarket shelves do have a few kinds of cereal like porridge oats, 'Weetabix' and

'Allbran'. Even 'Special K' which is seen as a slimming product in the UK, has chocolate chunks in it.

Again, biscuits are largely eaten by children, although there are a few 'posh' ones for adults. When children come home from school, they have a *'goûter'* – something to eat. It can be a piece of bread with a chunk of (milk) chocolate. Another term you might come across when kids come home from school is *'casse-croûte'* – a snack break.

Of course, Anglophones are quite keen on biscuits with their tea and the supermarkets do stock the most common varieties.

Interestingly, in our local supermarket, if you buy McVities digestives from the normal biscuit shelf, they are in a special box with *'Sablé Anglais'* written on the side. The same product, weight for weight (400g), is sold on the British counter, without the box, for a significantly higher price. This price difference has been the case for several years now. Note, if you shop online only the *'Sablé Anglais'* is listed. Weetabix is another product which is double the price on "British" shelf.

Some American recipes call for Graham Crackers, and the question is always what to use instead as they are not easily available in France. Since Graham crackers are made from Graham flour, which is a coarsely ground whole-wheat flour, then the simple answer is to use Digestives, *'Sable Anglais',* mentioned above, which are also made using course brown wheat flour. However, even easier to find are Speculoos, plain but slightly sweet/spiced Dutch biscuits, but they are not made with whole-wheat flour.

Meat & Fish

- Lard
- Suet
- Bacon
- Ham/Gammon
- English/French cuts of Meat
- Beef
- Sausages
- Saucisson
- Pork
- Lamb
- Poultry
- Fish

Lard – '*saindoux*'

Known as '*saindoux*' sometimes stocked in the chiller section near the cold meats/charcuterie, bacon '*poitrine*' and '*lardons*'.

Suet

It's possible you might find Atora beef suet and vegetarian suet on the British shelf in some larger supermarkets, but the usual advice is to either use cold/frozen grated butter or go to a butcher and ask for '*suif des rognons de bœuf*' and grate your own.

Bacon – *'poitrine'*

English style back bacon is not generally known here unless carried as a special item, usually frozen in the *'étranger'* section, or sometimes it can be found in Noz (a destocking supermarket where you can find bargains of all kinds). The nearest thing is either very thinly-cut streaky bacon *'poitrine'* – smoked *'poitrine fumée'* or unsmoked *'nature'*. Some brands are sweeter than others and so burn even more easily in the pan. Sometimes you will find very thickly cut poitrine, or further cut into dice/matchsticks and called *'lardons'*. You can still buy poitrine as a piece. It needs a very sharp knife to convert into bacon for sandwiches, but if you get it on the deli counter, they will slice it to whatever thickness you like. Thankfully this is still good and doesn't leak white water grunge into the pan when fried. It is also possible to find very round bacon, that looks as if cut from what would be the eye of back bacon. It is lean, artificially rounded, very thin and often has sugar added to the cure which makes it burn very easily.

The thinly cut '*poitrine*' that comes in plastic sachets is sometimes referred to as 'pancetta' but is unsmoked. It essentially the same product but comes from Italy.

Ham/gammon

Ham is called '*jambon*' which is divided into two groups. The first group is '*jambon cru*' which is a dried, smoked or cured product, which comes in many varieties which the French are immensely proud of and is used sliced very thinly in charcuterie dishes and not normally cooked further.

The kind of ham better known in the UK is called '*Jambon de Paris*' or '*Jambon Blanc*', and this is cooked. You can buy it as 'formed', precooked and thinly sliced in plastic packets, but you cannot seem to buy, for example, gammon joints for boiling or roasting at home. You will find whole gammons, hot, on the bone being sliced for sale in the motorway '*autoroute*' cafes, and very good it is too. But you will not find it in supermarkets to cook at home. The nearest thing is rather miserable ham hock/shank known as '*jarret*'. These have just about enough meat on them for a meagre meal for two and the stock can be used for making lentil soup, but that's about it. Something to bring back with you.

In fact, it is getting harder to find in the UK as most "gammon" joints appear to be formed with added water, but if you can overlook this, they are good value for money.

English – French cuts of meat - beef/lamb/pork

There are lots of sites you can find using Google or Bing which have diagrams showing the animal and French/English equivalent cuts. The only problem is that they are not exactly the same. French butchers cut somewhat differently - often along the muscle, rather than across it. The French are quite good at indicating on the displayed items what they are intended for - grilling, stewing, roasting etc

Beef – 'bœuf'

Minced beef is sold with various percentages of fat – e.g. 5%, 10%, 15% or 20%.

Faux filet - Sirloin - (not false nets!)

Paleron - à mijoter - Chuck to simmer

Bavette - a popular cut in France. It is fibrous and chewy and can be packed with flavour, but it's vital that the meat is cut very thinly across the grain, grilled on a high heat and it is at its best when cooked medium-rare.

The French like their meat cooked much less than in the UK or USA, unless it is cooked for a very long time as in a daub or stew, because it isn't hung for long, and becomes very tough if 'bien cuit'.

Recently well-hung beef has become popular in high end Parisian restaurants, with prices which reflect the fact that the butchers must hang it for a few weeks, or even longer.

French terminology 'doness' of meat.

English	French	Temp.	Meat Colour	Juice Colour
Very blue	Très bleu	45°C	Original colour	Dark red
Blue	Bleu	55°C	Red	Red
Medium rare	Saignant	60°C	Rosé	Pink
Medium well	A point	65°C	Pinkish brown	Clear
Well done	Bien cuit	70°C	Brown	No juice

Sausages

Likewise, sausages in France are 100% meat, so many of us who are used to various fillers like rusk may not be keen on the different texture of 100% meat sausages. Typically, in supermarkets, on the fresh meat counters, you will find Toulouse sausages and the thinner and longer chipolatas. Pork, veal and beef are all used. There are many flavourings too. 'Saucisses' is the word used here for sausages which are usually cooked and eaten hot.

Saucisson

In the UK it is possible to buy chorizo, salami and several other dried and cured sausages but in France 'saucisson' reaches another level altogether. *Saucisson* is a product of what is termed as '*charcuterie*' and is made up of a minced meat of one or more varieties of meat, mainly pork, which is seasoned in many ways according to

local, regional or national traditions. After being put into a natural or artificial casing, the sausage is either "steamed and/or dried", sometimes smoked for at least four weeks, or "steamed and/or poached" and then cooled in a broth, e.g. garlic sausage. Its diameter can be from a few millimetres to about twenty centimetres, and anything from, normally 15 to 30 centimetres long, but can be much longer as shown in the photo from a summer display in our local supermarket. Saucisson is sold in its entirety, in sections or slices under all kinds of names.

Pork

Normally you will find pork without its rind and with most of the fat trimmed off, so it is not possible to have roast pork with crackling. Sometimes the big supermarkets hold a *'Foire au porc'*, when you can buy a half or a quarter of a pig at a knock down price, and usually the rind is left on these. The alternative is to buy the pork rind which is sold separately and called *'couenne'*, it's in neat little packets rolled up. You can then stick this on your joint with cocktail sticks and it will crackle. The French value the *'couenne'* for soup making and for flavouring

vegetables like tinned haricot beans. If you go to the butchers, you can ask for a joint with the rind left on – for example: *'épaule de porc avec couenne'* – shoulder of pork with the rind.

Lamb

French lamb is not my favourite. Expensive and with little taste, even the organic *'bio'* kind. This may be a regional thing as I have heard some folk compare French lamb favourably with Welsh lamb. You don't find it minced either. What you can find is legs of frozen New Zealand lamb in the supermarkets, which is usually very reasonably priced and good quality.

Poultry

Chicken *'poulet'*, duck *'canard'* and turkey *'dinde'* are available in all supermarkets, as well as street markets. If you buy a chicken in the market, and sometimes in a supermarket, it will come with its head, and with luck, its other giblets for making gravy. In French supermarkets, chicken thighs *'cuisses de poulet'* tend to come with a portion of the backbone *'os'*, whereas, chicken thighs from the big German supermarkets (Aldi and Lidl) come without the backbone, so are easier to prepare. Chicken livers tend to be sold in small plastic pots and gizzards *'gésiers'* are sold in tins, or vacuum packed – very popular sliced into a salad. Take care not to mistake *'poulet'* and *'poule'*. The latter are old birds sold for making soup and are a bit tough and tasteless if you make the mistake of roasting them.

Duck

Duck, if not sold whole, is generally separated into breasts– *'magret de canard'* (sometimes this is dried and smoked, – *'séché et fumé'*), and sometimes the inner squab of breast is sold as *'Aiguillettes'* which are good used in stir-fries, and are usually cheaper than the main part of the breast. The legs *'cuisses de canard'* - often these come as *'cuisses de canard confit'* – i.e. duck legs (thigh and drumstick) marinated in salt and herbs and then simmered very slowly in duck fat and either tinned or vacuum-packed in duck fat. *Confit de manchons de canard* is the same as *cuisses de canard confit* but made with the top of the wing and a small portion of the breast, which some folks mistakenly think is the drumstick from the picture on the can. *Manchons* are about half the price of the *cuisses,* however.

Custard-coloured, raw, *'foie gras'* comes whole vacuum packed in the chiller cabinet generally, in the autumn, when you will also see duck carcasses *'isabelles'* for sale very cheaply for making soup or stock.

'Foie gras'

'Foie Gras' or fattened liver was discovered by the Egyptians when they observed migratory birds like ducks or geese, naturally overfeeding to endure winter and flying long distances. Nowadays this process is given a helping hand resulting in a product that is still very popular in France. You will find it in several forms:

Raw *'foie gras'* is generally cut into slices, and simply flash fried before being served. To the amateur it is very easy to overcook it and end up with a panful of melted fat.

Foie gras *'mi-cuit'* - semi-cooked. It is cooked at 80°C and can be kept for 6 months at a temperature of 0°C to 4°C. It is available in terrines, jars or tins.

Preserved foie gras is sterilised, cooked to between 105° and 115°. It may be stored for some years.

Foie gras is served at the beginning of the meal, as an entree or appetiser with a glass of sweet Monbazillac wine, which is said to be the only accompaniment to adequately complement the dish. (Pronounced: mon-baz-ee-ac).

Foie gras is delicious with a sweet chutney made with figs or onions and is often served up in the centre of a terrine which may be served after the soup course on many menus.

'Rillettes'

'Rillettes' is somewhat like pâté. Often made from pork, but also duck and goose *'oie'*, the meat is chopped, salted heavily and cooked slowly in fat, shredded, and then cooled with enough of the fat to form a paste. *Rillette* is spread on bread or toast and served at room temperature. (Pronounced: ree – yet)

Turkey

Turkey *'dinde'* is cheap and normally sold cut up, but at Christmas it is possible to find small whole turkeys, but they are not as popular a choice as in the UK or USA. On Christmas Eve – *'veille de Noël'* (when they celebrate Christmas), the French prefer to eat shellfish – oysters *'huitres'* are hugely popular, and you can buy lobster *'homard'*, langoustines and a huge selection of other fish.

Mini-dictionary– meat products

English	French
Lard	Saindoux
Streaky bacon – smoked or unsmoked	Poitrine – fumée or nature
Cooked ham	Jambon de Paris / jambon blanc
Ham – raw / dried	Jambon cru / sec
Turkey	Dinde
Chicken/old chicken	Poulet/poule
Chicken Thigh (includes drumstick)	Cuisses de Poulet
Duck thigh – as above	Cuisses de canard
Duck wings (after sleeve)	Manchons de canard
Gizzard – meaty stomach muscle of poultry	Gésier
Bone	Os
Duck breast	Magret de canard
Duck leg simmered and stored in duck fat	Cuisses de canard confit
Duck or goose liver (literally fat liver)	Foie gras
Pork skin/rind	Couenne

English/French fish and crustacea

If you start talking to someone French about fish bones, perhaps asking what 'fish bones' are called in French, they will be puzzled, because they are not thought of as 'bones'. They are *'arêtes de poisson'*.

In France there is often a north-south divide when it comes to names. For example – *'sac'* or *'poche'* for bag, or *'chocolatine'* or *'pain au chocolate'* for a similar confection. Similarly, there is confusion over what to ask for when buying fish.

If you see *'colin'* it may be hake, but equally if you see *'merlu'*, that might be hake.

Pollack may also be called *'colin'*. Pollack can be sold as *'lieu jeune'* with coley sold as *'lieu noir'*.

Sea bass has several names on French menus. You might see it as *Bar, Bar Commun, Bar Sauvage* or *Bar de Ligne*. In the South you might see it as *Loup* or *Loup de Mer,* or closer to Spain you might see the Spanish name *Lubina*.

Monkfish (Angler Fish or Goosefish) is one of the tastiest of all sea fish with succulent, very firm, very white meat; in France you might find it as *Lotte, Lotte de Mer, Gigot de Mer, Diable de Mer, Baudroie, Baudroie Commune*.

John Dory comes from the French Jaune Dore, meaning golden yellow, and that is this fish's colour when freshly caught. The French names *Saint-Pierre* or *San-Pierre* refers to the characteristic eye mark on their side that is said to be the thumbprint of St Peter, who pulled one out of the sea on Jesus's command.

If you see *'amande'* on a seafood menu they are probably referring to *Amande de Mer, Amande Marbrée*, but it may be just to the almonds used in the cooking. The sea almond or dog cockle is a clam which is often on French seafood platters.

Cockles in French are *'Coques'*. In French the word coque also means shell. So, on French menus, the word coque may also be used for *'œuf à la coque'*, boiled eggs, *crabe préparé en coque*, crab prepared in its shell, etc.

Gambas is used mostly for very large prawns. Shrimps, prawns and *gambas* are all kinds of *crevette*. What the American call shrimps, the British call prawns.

Crevette rose - prawn

Crevette grise - shrimp (smaller than prawn)

Ecrevisse – crayfish (smaller than lobsters)

Langoustine - a large prawn or small lobster – Dublin bay prawn.

Noix de Saint-Jacques means the nut or meat of the scallop. A menu listing *Coquille Saint-Jacques* means the scallop will be served in its shell.

Cabillaud is the name for Fresh Cod, *Morue* is re-hydrated salt cod. On French menus *Morue de l'Atlantique, Morue Fraîche*, and *Morue Franche*. This is the very popular reconstituted, dried and salted cod. In pre-refrigeration times dried and salted cod was a massive industry; it existed for hundreds of years, and in a reduced scale it still exists today. *Brandade de Morue* is one of the most popular traditional dishes made with re-hydrated and desalted cod.

Mini-dictionary - fish

Fish	Poisson
Anchovies	Anchois
Barracuda	Barracuda bécune
Black bream	Dorade gris
Brill	Barbue
Brown crab	Tourteau or Dormeur
Cod (fresh, not salted)	Cabillaud
Cod salted	Morue
Conger	Congre
Crayfish	Écrevisse
Cuttlefish	Seiche
Dab (plaice family)	Limande
Dog Fish	Roussette
Eel	Anguille
Fish bone	Arête de poisson
Fish steak	Darnes de poison

Fish	Poisson
Haddock	Églefin
Hake (see also Colin)	Merlu
Hake (see also Merlu)	Colin
Large prawn	Gambas
Lemon sole	Limande sole
Like a small clam	Palourdes
Ling (type of Cod)	Julienne
Lobster	Homard
Monkfish	Lotte
Oyster	Huître
Perch	Perche
Pike	Brochet
Plaice	Carrelet or Plie
Pollack	Lieu Jaune
Pollock	Goberge / Lieu Noir
Rainbow trout	Truite Arc-en-Ciel

Fish	Poisson
Red bream	Dorade commune
Red Mullet	Rouget Barbet/de Roche
Salmon	Saumon
Saltwater crayfish	Langoustine
Scallop	Coquille St. Jacques
Sea bass	Bar Bass
Sea bass	Perche de mer
Sea bream	Daurade
Shark	Requin
Shellfish	Crustacés
Shrimp brown/large	Crevette gris /grosse
Skate	Aigle de mer
Skate wing	Aile de Raie
Spider crab	Araignée de mer
Squid	Calamars
Sturgeon	Esturgeon

Fish	Poisson
Sword Fish	Espadon
Trout/ Brown Trout	Truite/ Truite Fario
Tuna	Thon
Type of clam	Amandes de mer
Whelk	Bulot
Whitebait/fried smelt	Friture/friture d'éperlan
Whiting	Merlan
Young pike	Brocheton
Zander	Sandre

Culinary weights and measures

Cuillère à soupe

Recipes on French packets of food, in French magazines etc, always refer to *'cuillère à soupe'* 'soup spoons' rather than tablespoons, which for me has been rather confusing. In fact, both are 15ml.

Hoorah for the French decimal system, which makes everything clear and unambiguous!

Several French people have looked at me condescendingly and said it's obvious that a soupspoon is the same as a tablespoon. Maybe it speaks volumes about my background, but at home a tablespoon was always used on the table for serving vegetables. A soupspoon, with a rounded bowl, was used for eating (slurping) soup. A dessertspoon was about the same size as a soupspoon, with a more elongated bowl, was used to eat dessert, unless it was something like ice cream in which case if we didn't have fancy knickerbocker glory spoons, we used teaspoons, which were most often found in the saucer of our teacups for stirring in sugar. Smaller than those are coffee spoons which reflect the fact that after-dinner coffee was taken from very small coffee cups. A French coffee spoon, however, is equivalent to an English teaspoon 5ml.

With recipes easily available on the internet, one of the biggest sources of confusion is the way we measure things, and it's not just spoons. I realise that American readers will know about the following, but for British cooks coming to France, and perhaps using the internet for recipes more than ever, the use of 'cups' for measuring ingredients is very confusing.

American pints to millilitres

American liquid measures use the same terminology as the old imperial measures used until recently in UK, but the volumes are confusingly different. An American fluid ounce is the same as an Imperial Fluid ounce. But an American pint is only 16 fluid ounces whereas an imperial pint is 20 fluid ounces, which means quarts and gallons are not the same in the 2 systems. You need to be aware of this when trying to convert a recipe to millilitre or decilitres.

American cups to grams

Americans use 'cups' to measure liquid and dry products. Very confusing to a British person who will sit there thinking what size cup? A coffee cup? Teacup? A mug? Does it matter? (The British do have 'cups'. These are any old cup you take to your next-door neighbour when you've run out of something and ask to borrow a cup of flour/sugar or whatever.)

From a set of measuring spoons purchased in UK we have:

1 tablespoon (tbsp) = 15 ml

1 teaspoon (tsp) = 5 ml

½ teaspoon = 2.5 ml

¼ teaspoon = 1.25 ml

From a set of cups purchased in USA we have the following liquid measures:

1 cup = 250 ml = 8fl oz

½ cup = 125 ml = 4fl oz

⅓ cup = 80 ml = 3fl oz

¼ cup = 60 ml = 2fl oz

American recipes seem to make life super easy by measuring everything, liquid or solid by cups. Unfortunately, a cup of flour doesn't weigh the same as a cup of sugar. So, if you have an American recipe you want to use in France, and do not have a set of American measuring cups you are going to have to spend some time looking up the metric equivalents for each product.

Note that many recipes will give you gram/cup equivalents. You shouldn't mix and match because they will have often adjusted the recipe quantities in the search for a more sensible range of measures – nothing worse than measuring out 113g of this and 128g of that to make both sets of measurements exactly equivalent.

If you don't have a set of American cups, but you do have a measuring jug with fluid ounces on the side, then you can measure up to the 8oz mark to get a cup, and the 4 oz mark to get half a cup.

N.B. 1 stick or 1/2 cup butter is equal to 4 ounces, or 113 grams.

N.B.

Shops selling en vrac products, now by law must accept containers from home if they are "fit for purpose" this includes liquids. Just make sure they are see-through, otherwise you could end up with an embarrassing mess!

Household

- Cleaning products
- Bleach
- Eparcyl and fosse septiques
- Paper Products

Cleaning Products

It is surprising what you can still buy in the way of chemicals in

supermarkets and hardware stores here. Items such as spirits of salt / hydrochloric acid / '*Acide Chlorhydrique*', are usually stocked among the cleaning products where you also find white vinegar, acetone etc. The bigger supermarkets stock them as well as the DIY stores like Leroy Merlin; Mr Bricolage or Bricomarché.

Many of the products are sold in different strengths, although the solutions have been weakened, and some *bio* substitutes are appearing on the market.

Ammonia '*ammoniaque alcali*', washing soda '*lessive de soude*', walnut stain '*Brou de noix*' and turpentine '*térébenthine*' are all shown in the photo and methylated spirits below.

ACTION, (a store from Holland originally, sells many diverse things, such as light bulbs and memory cards very cheaply), have a very good range of bio cleaning products which generally work well. It's a UK company that make them, so instructions are all in English. Very often products sold in France have many other languages on their instruction/ingredient labels, but not English. This is also a good place to buy Matt "Wall Colour" paint. It comes in white or cream, is half the price of other local paint, made from recycled products and covers twice as well.

Bleach

Bleach is known as *'Eau de Javel'*.

Once you have purchased a plastic container of Javel, you can

purchase concentrated refills as shown at the top of the photo. This is both cheaper and saves on the amount of single use plastic.

Javel is also available in tablet form.

Eparcyl and Fosse septique

If you have a septic tank '*fosse septique*' you will often be advised to flush a packet of 'eparcyl' down the toilet each week. If your septic tank

is working properly this is not necessary, and I stopped using it years ago with no ill effect. However, if yours is a '*maison secondaire*' (holiday home), empty for much of the time, then 'eparcyl' may be just what you need to get the bugs working again. You should also use a toilet cleaner that is adapted for septic tanks and avoid flushing anything but the 3 'P's – no wet wipes, tampons or teddy bears!

Lovers of Fairy Liquid, you can get it here in an identical bottle from 'Perigordine' (an agricultural co-op) under the name of Proctor & Gamble 'Dreft' (yep, I know that is the name for a product to wash woollens in the UK).

Paper products

As you would expect, supermarkets stock a wide range of paper, envelopes and office supplies.

One thing you won't find is lined pads. The French use squared paper, rather like that once used in British schools for maths.

Another big difference between the UK and France is that there is no tradition of sending Christmas cards, although you can find some greeting cards.

As well as paper napkins and paper tablecloths, the French like to use tough flexible plastic cloths to protect their tables, and this you can buy off the roll, in shops, markets and fabric shops. The sight of these cheerful decorative, but practical coverings for tables in the kitchen and outside is something that really marks you as being in France. This is not something you will find in the UK.

If you want to purchase art supplies, one of the main places to look is in the various DIY or 'BRICO' stores! Other than that 'Action' and 'Centrakor' both do cheap art supplies, and LeClerc Cultura do art materials as well.

FROM POTAGER TO POT

Recipes for dealing with your garden produce

In this section I list the fruit and vegetables that come from my potager and give you some idea of what to do with all the bounty you may have. If you don't have a garden, then some of these ideas may be useful if you buy the 1€ boxes of outdated produce *'anti-gaspillage'* from Lidl and then wonder what to do with the excess courgettes or lettuce. Similarly, the markets sometimes practically give away tomatoes at the end of the day. In rural areas especially, an astonishing amount of fruit goes to waste, just rotting under trees, and if that is what happens in your garden, then, if you're like me it is hard to just leave it there, although the local wild-life may well be pleased. On the other hand, if you want to keep the wild boar, *'sanglier'*, and deer out of your garden, then disposing of apples and other fruit is essential, as is some form of suitable fence. It must be pretty high to keep out deer, and strong enough to keep out the *sanglier*. We've used electric fences in the garden to keep out the *sanglier*, but it must be powerful enough, at least two joules, ours is 4 joules. A lot of those driven by solar power are not up to the job.

Agretti

The green fronds of agretti were once sought across Europe to be reduced to ashes for use in making glass. These days, the verdant Italian plant is once more in demand as a vegetable traditionally served with oil and lemon. It is also very good baked in a quiche.

Agretti is difficult to find in shops, so if you want to eat it you have no choice but to grow your own. Otherwise known as saltwort or friar's beard – or "land seaweed", in Japan – agretti has a short early-summer seasonal window.

The seed, which has a shelf life of barely six months and a germination rate of about 30 per cent is also difficult to find, so once you are growing it the best thing is to let one plant grow to maturity

and allow it to drop its seeds in the potager, from whence new plants will grow the following year.

Asparagus - *asperge*

Asparagus is something the French really love - as do the British. The English like the green varieties best and the French seem to go for the white blanched varieties. There is always a lot available in the markets and supermarkets, and both bottled and fresh are popular.

Fresh asparagus is available from early March to late June, their availability extended by imports.

There are three varieties of asparagus:

White: harvested as soon as it comes out of the ground, it is

cultivated in Alsace and Belgium and is imported from North Africa. Large and soft, it does not have much taste. It is grown under black plastic to keep the light out.

Violet: harvested when it has emerged a few centimetres. It comes from Aquitaine, the Charentes, the Loire, but also from Italy; it is delicious and very fruity.

Green: picked when it measures about fifteen centimetres. Many say this is the most delicious of all.

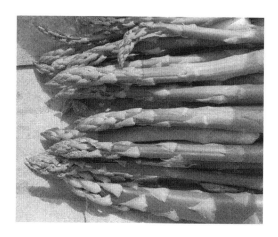

There are also wild asparagus, thin and green, slightly bitter but very good.

One thing is for sure, folks may not want your excess apples or plums, but nobody ever turns away a gift of asparagus.

Preparing and cooking asparagus

Of course, asparagus is delicious just served with a good hollandaise sauce, or grilled with fried quail's eggs on top, or in a host of ways you'll find on the internet. It's important not to overcook it (not more than approx. 5 minutes), and if you can get one of those tall narrow pots so that the bottom can cook under water and the fragile tops just sit above in the steam, so much the better. Of course, young tasty, freshly cut asparagus will cook more quickly than old which might have been sitting on the supermarket shelf for a few days. Also, old asparagus tends to need peeling as it gets bitter and tough. When its fresh and young there is no need to peel. Make sure you cut off the bottom woody part of the asparagus spears. They will break at the appropriate point if you bend them.

Like sweetcorn and fresh peas, freshly picked asparagus beats day-old asparagus hands down and has to be one of the main reasons for growing it yourself.

Artichokes – 'Artichaut' & Jerusalem Artichoke – 'Topinambour'

Popular vegetables in France are artichokes – both the globe and the 'Jerusalem/girasole' or 'sunchoke' variety. The French enjoy cooked globe artichokes dipped in hollandaise sauce, butter or vinaigrette, and equally enjoy them from a tin, and they also enjoy palm hearts, unavailable in the UK.

Globe artichokes come in several varieties and are easy to grow but being British I find them a lot of work for not much reward and tend to let them flower, which is great news for the bees.

The reason for writing about these two plants together other than the confusing English naming is that the both contain inulin giving them a similar sweet taste, but the root vegetable has about one and a half times as much inulin as the globe artichoke, which for many people creates a distressing amount of wind.

Jerusalem artichokes are extremely invasive. In America they are known as sunchokes because they are related to the sunflower and have a yellow flower and grow as tall. They are also a pain to clean and prepare but are delicious in soup or roasted.

Topinambour

Broad beans

Broad beans *'fèves'* are one of those vegetable that you rarely find young enough on a market or in the supermarket, so the only way to get them small and fresh enough is to grow them. I recently found some frozen, skinned (with their inner skins removed). When I cooked them, they were disappointingly ordinary, and then when used up in soup there was an overpowering taste of mint (!).

What I've found, growing broad beans on my south facing potager in the Dordogne, is that I need to sow the seed before Christmas, in order to get a decent crop. I find that planting them in Spring is too late and the crop is disappointing.

I've usually grown a variety called Aquadulce, but recently found 'Wizard Field Beans' which are smaller more robust relatives of broad beans. The beans are about 1/2 the size of a normal broad bean and the plants are full size (taller than me 1.75m), bearing huge numbers of pods with 3 or 4 seed packed closely together. The overall effect is usually a higher yield of beans from the same size plot.

'Wizard' is a modern pale-skinned variety which has been bred for table use and is very hardy, surviving over harsh winters when others die off.

It has a particularly good flavour even when the seeds mature, and does very well everywhere, cropping over a longer period than broad beans.

Broadbean tops

The usual advice is to remove the top 7 cm of the plants once the beans start to form to reduce the risk of black fly. Assuming the black fly haven't already infested the plants, these soft succulent leaves make great eating either in a salad or cooked as a green.

The beans themselves I pick quite small, shell, blanche and freeze immediately apart from those I eat on the day of picking.

Capers

Capers (Capparis spinosa) are a fun plant to grow, if you have a very dry stony spot. You can pick and pickle the buds, but they also have very beautiful white flowers with magenta stamens, which of course you lose if you pickle the flower buds.

As the Latin name implies capers are very spiny so picking capers

can be quite a painful process. Like olives caper buds are very bitter, so take some processing to remove the bitterness. So, for those reasons, and because the flowers are so pretty, it is probably preferable to pickle nasturtiums seeds which taste and look remarkably similar once pickled.

Pickled Nasturtium Seeds

Ingredients

- 200g of nasturtium seeds
- Brine made from 2tbs salt to 250ml water
- 300ml of white wine vinegar[7] or cider vinegar
- 2 tsp sugar
- 2 bay leaves and 1 sprig thyme

Method

1. Soak the nasturtium seeds in brine for 3 days, then
2. Boil up 300ml vinegar sugar, bay leaves and thyme, and
3. Pour over the drained nasturtium seeds.
4. Store, covered with vinegar, in a jar in the fridge for up to 6 months.

---

[7] I have found it almost impossible to find plain white wine vinegar in France. You see plenty of white wine vinegars flavoured with shallot or tarragon. You also find a balsamic version of white wine vinegar.

Citrus – '*agrumes*'

I brought some small citrus trees (now a lot bigger) with me to France; gifts from the kids over the years which I used to keep outside over the winter. You will see a lot of citrus for sale in supermarkets and garden shops here. They do quite well here, outside, but dislike being brought in for the winter. But unless you live in the very south, they need to be brought in, because it can get too cold for them outside. We've experienced -19°C just once, but as low as -10°C not infrequently.

The temperature that citrus can tolerate varies. If temperatures are going to fall below 4°C, except briefly, then I bring mine in. Depending on the variety, they can tolerate -3°C /-4°C. In their natural habitat, these shrubs grow in understorey, well sheltered from the winds by the surrounding vegetation. In France they need a lot of sunshine in order to fruit. Indoors ideally, they need a bright and airy place, which is not too warm: a veranda or an orangery is perfect. Many of us do not have the ideal place. Too dark, too hot, too dry and they will lose their leaves, but all is not lost, if you are not too neglectful, they will revive when you take them out again. But watch out, because they are understorey

plants the leaves will tend to be scorched by the sun, especially those nice tender new shoots and leaves that developed whilst they were indoors.

Citrus like acidic soil and don't like their feet in water. You don't need to water them much in winter but don't let them dry out either. You can give them some ash from your wood burner and spent coffee grounds will help to keep bugs away. They are susceptible to getting a range of bugs whilst indoors. My particular bane are scale insects, which are almost impossible to get rid of. The moment you see any destroy them using thumb nail and methylated spirits *'d'alcool à brûler'* or *'alcool de méthyle'*. Spray the tree with *'savon noir'* (black soap made from olive oil) and follow that with neem oil. Scale insects multiply quickly and ruin your fruit, especially if you want to use the zest.

Kumquats

Kumquats are small and full of pips. We've used them to make liqueur, a bit like limoncello, but they also make great marmalade, and although a bit of a fuss, you can make candied kumquats, and they are delicious.

Candied Kumquats

Ingredients:

- About 1kg fresh kumquats
- 200g sugar, plus more for coating the kumquats
- 500ml water
- Pinch salt
- Pinch of cream of tartar

Method

1. Wash and check over the kumquats. Prick the kumquats all over (at least 10 times) with a pin or skewer.

2. Place them in a large saucepan and cover with water. Bring the water to the boil, then allow to cool for half an hour, drain the water, replace and bring to the boil again, and do this a third time. You can leave the fruit until the next day at this stage.

3. Put the kumquats back in the pan, add the sugar, 500ml water, salt, and cream of tartar, bring the pot to the boil, and then lower the heat to a slow simmer as the kumquats will be very tender at this point and will easily fall apart. Slowly cook the fruit until the fruit looks translucent and dark (about an hour). Cover the pan and let the fruit sit overnight in the syrup. Bring to the boil, leave to cool – three times over – until they look like balls of pure amber

4. Thoroughly drain the kumquats. (reserve the syrup) leave to drain on a cake rack overnight. Next day roll the sticky kumquats, a few at a time, in some caster sugar until they are completely coated. These should keep in an airtight container layered with more sugar but in my experience the sugared kumquats go deliquescent, so it is probably better not to roll them in sugar until shortly before you need them. Use while still plump and fresh.

5. The reserved syrup can be used over pancakes or ice-cream, or as a delicious coating for things like baked ham. The kumquats are delicious just eaten as sweet treats but can also be cut up and used to decorate ice-cream, syllabub or other desserts.

Lemons - *citron*

My lemon tree has spines, but not as many as the lime. I think it is quite an ugly tree, but the fruit does come in handy when cooking and jam making. Sometimes I leave the lemons on the tree too long and you find the seeds are sprouting into new trees when you cut them open. As well as using in gin and tonic, you can make lemon curd, or even better, limoncello.

Limoncello

Ingredients:

- 200g caster sugar
- 150ml water
- zest and juice of 6 unwaxed lemons
- 700ml '*eau-de-vie*' (colourless fruit liqueur you can buy here in supermarkets like Intermarché), or you could use vodka

Method:

1. Dissolve the sugar in the water, bring to the boil, and simmer for 3-4 minutes until the bubbles look syrupy. Leave to cool.

2. Wash the lemons, zest them and add zest and juice to the syrup while it is still slightly warm. Then add the '*eau-de-vie*' or vodka. Leave in a large sterile jar for 7 days to infuse, shaking daily.

3. Pour into sterile bottles or jars, seal and label prettily.

4. Before serving put in the freezer for several hours and serve in frozen shot glasses.

Limes – *citron vert*

For me the best accompaniment for a gin and tonic is a slice of lime. Preferably the gin should be kept in the fridge or freezer, as should the tonic (which must not be slim line). Always buy the best quality tonic you can. The quinine used to flavour tonic is a very expensive ingredient and is the first thing that gets cut back in cheap tonics. There are lots of different tonics out there these days, and lots of different gins, but all can be ruined by being served with warm, flat tonic. Ideally don't use tonic from large plastic bottles – it only goes flat and ruins your drink. If you do have any flat tonic, then make ice-cubes out of it for your drink rather than diluting your it with ordinary ice. If you end up with more limes than you can use in gin and tonic, you could slice them up and freeze ready for future drinks, or you can use to make a zingy lime marmalade, or lime-cello.

One of our favourites is to use them with some Seville oranges to make a 'Citrus Marmalade. Seville oranges are known as '*Oranges Amères*' in France and are available from late December until early February. You can get them in places like Grand Frais, or sometimes at the Biocoop.

Orange *Amère* and Lime Marmalade

I think of this as a 2 days process.

After washing the fruit, you need to cook it whole for maybe three-quarters of an hour to soften the peel. The peel will never go soft once it is in contact with sugar, so take as long as you need to get this first stage right. I usually do it the day before and let it all cool down overnight.

With the wide-based pot that I use for *'confiture'* (jam) making slightly under 2kgs of fruit covers the bottom of the pot in a single layer. You need about 2.75 litres of water to cover the fruit. Turn the fruit over halfway through cooking.

You will need enough jars and lids for 7kg of marmalade - about 15 depending on size, which you will sterilise just before bottling your marmalade. I do this by rewashing them and putting them on a tray in the oven for 15 minutes at 120°C and boiling the lids for 10 minutes.

Ingredients:

- 2kg Seville oranges or oranges and limes mixed
- 2 large lemons
- 2.8 litres water
- *'Sucre cristal'* - this comes in 5kg bags

Method

1. If you buy in any of the fruit make sure you scrub it in hot soapy water to get the wax coating off, and in any case wash the fruit to remove all dust and dirt.

2. Cook the whole fruit as mentioned above. The fruit is ready when a knife pierces the orange/lime skin with little

resistance. Take off the heat, keep the lid on and allow to cool preferably overnight.

3. Keep all the cooking water. Cut the fruit in half and scoop out the flesh with a spoon and fork. Add the pulp and juice to the cooking water but put all the pips into a small muslin jelly bag (a lot of the pectin is around the seeds).

4. Slice the fruit skins into strips as thick or thin as you like.

5. Add the shredded skin to the reserved juice and measure. For each 500ml of this mixture, you will need one 400g of sugar.

6. Return the prepared fruit mix to the saucepan and add the sugar, add the bag full of pips - tied up so they won't get out into the marmalade. Bring to a rolling boil and boil for 30 minutes only.

7. After 30 minutes the marmalade should be setting. Temperature 104.5C or put a drop of jelly on a chilled saucer and hold the saucer vertically. If the drop stays put it is ready, if it 'slips' it is not cooked enough, so give it another 5 minutes if need be, but the longer it cooks the darker it will get.

8. When it is ready, let the marmalade stand for 15 minutes before potting to help with even distribution of peel.

9. Stir and pour into sterilised jars and seal immediately

Lime pickle

Traditionally lime pickle takes quite a long time to make as it is put into jars and left in the sun to mature over a period of weeks. However, it is possible to make a good pickle in just an hour or two, and this is an excellent way of using up some of your excess limes.

Ingredients

- 500g of chillies (a mix of red and green)
- 1kg limes
- 200g fresh ginger
- 15 garlic cloves
- 6 fresh curry leaves
- 1 litre white vinegar
- 1 tsp turmeric
- 1 tbsp salt
- 3 tbsp mustard seed
- 2 tbsp fenugreek seeds
- 750ml vegetable oil (If you have mustard oil, use 500ml vegetable oil and 250ml mustard oil)
- 5 tbsp vegetable oil

Preparation:

Make sure you have sterilised jars and lids prepared for bottling. They must be thoroughly dried!

Method

1. Heat 3 tbsp of oil in a large frying pan until hot.

2. Sauté the limes turning them over until their skins are a golden brown.

3. Dry the limes and cut them into about 6 thick slices and then half the slices.

4. Put 2 tbsp of oil into a blender, add the chillies, garlic, ginger and curry leaves. Blend to a paste

5. Heat the remaining oil in a pan until hot. Add mustard and fenugreek. Heat the seeds until they pop.

6. Add the paste, stir and simmer for 15 minutes. Turn off heat.

7. Add the turmeric, pieces of lime and vinegar and stir until thoroughly mixed.

8. Using a slotted ladle or spoon, put the limes into jars, and pour the remaining fluid over the limes ensuring they are just covered.

9. Stir to remove any air bubbles and seal jars.

The lime pickle can be eaten immediately, but it improves with age.

Chillies

I grow chillies because I love them, and they are hard to buy in France. Sometimes you see them with Christmas treats in the supermarket, and Grand Frais usually have the small bird eye chillies, but the kind you get in UK supermarkets for chopping up to drop on pizza, make a curry or any one of a dozen different dishes that require some spice, are almost impossible to find. The French tend not like spicy foods, although with the arrival of, and popularity of, junk food '*malbouffe*' or fast-food, tastes are changing rapidly in France.

The problem with growing chillies is that you end up with too many. You can freeze them, you can dry them, and blitz them to make your own chilli powder and you will still have too many. Here are a couple of recipes to help use up the glut:

Sweet Chilli dipping sauce

Ingredients

- 3 large cloves garlic
- 2 chillies
- 120g sugar
- 180ml water
- 60ml vinegar e.g. cider vinegar
- ½ tbsp salt
- 1 tbsp cornflour (Maizena)
- 2 tbsp water

Method:

1. Blend the first six ingredients – or at least chop the first 2 and then combine with the rest.

2. Put into a small saucepan, bring to the boil and simmer for 3 minutes until it starts to thicken.

3. Mix the cornflour and water into a slurry.

4. Whisk into the first mixture.

5. Bring it to a simmer again and cook for a further minute or so until it thickens, and all the chilli and garlic bits are held in suspension.

6. Pour into little dishes people can use for dipping – typically we like prawn crackers dipped in it.

7. It will store in the fridge in a glass jar for a couple of days, but best used up more-or-less immediately.

Something unusual you can do with green chillies is make Tequila Chillies. This recipe is from 'Sweets Made Simple'[8] Basically, once deseeded, the chillies are soaked overnight in alcohol, in this case tequila, (but you could use gin or grappa), then stuffed with a tequila, lime and white chocolate ganache, and finally coated with white chocolate, served as an after dinner sweet.

---

[8]https://www.bbc.com/food/recipes/tequila_chillies_40712)

One more popular recipe to use up your crab apples is to make crab apple and chilli jelly.

Crab Apple & Chilli Jelly

Ingredients

- 1.2kg of crab apples,
- 70g of chillies from the garden (cut into 3 or 4 pieces with seeds),
- 2 litres of water,
- Sugar – 400g for each half litre of strained juice
- 100ml cider vinegar

Method

1. Boil apples and chillies for about 3/4 hour till until mushy,
2. Strain overnight.
3. For each ½ litre of juice produced, add 400g sugar
4. Add 100ml cider vinegar
5. Boil until it reaches 104.5 degrees C. happens quite quickly as there is so much pectin in the crab apples.
6. Put into relatively small sterilised jars.

This is great with cheese and cold meats and makes a lovely present to anyone who likes something spicy.

Courgettes - zucchini

This is something else which is easy to grow in France, and easy to get too many of. We have two main ways of using them other than in 'Glutney' (See Pam Corbin's Preserves - chutney made with whatever glut you have).

We make a lot into courgette soup, a recipe we originally found in Lindsey Bareham's Celebration of Soup. We have experimented with the recipe, but her recipe remains the best.

Courgette soup

Ingredients

- 50g butter

- 1 small onion finely diced

- 1 shallot finely diced

- 900g courgettes chopped

- 1 cooked potato. It must be cooked, otherwise the soup goes like wallpaper paste. So, if you've only got a raw potato chop it small and fry it with the onion and shallot

- Salt & Pepper

- 1.75 litres stock

- 2 tbsp mint freshly chopped

- 2 tbsp parsley freshly chopped

Method

- Melt the butter in a pot and gently sweat the onion and shallot until transparent (adding finely diced potato if it isn't already cooked).

- Stir in chopped courgettes and potato (if not already added) and cook for about 5 minutes string from time to time.

- Add the stock, bring to the boil and simmer for 5 minutes or so. Liquidize with the mint and parsley, reheat briefly check seasoning and serve.

- This is quick, uses up a lot of courgettes and is a lovely fresh summer soup. We sometimes substitute coriander leaves for the mint, but mint is best. We've tried numerous variations with garlic, with all sorts of things, but the original is best.

Another way to use up some courgettes is to pickle them in a similar fashion to cucumber pickle.

Courgette pickle from the Real Seed Collection

Ingredients

- 1kg courgettes, washed and sliced 1-2mm thick
- 1/2 cup sugar
- 2 medium onions, sliced 1-2mm thick
- 1 tsp celery seed
- 1/2 cup salt
- 1 tsp mustard seed
- 2 1/2 cups white wine or cider vinegar
- 1 tsp turmeric

Method

1. Put the sliced courgettes and onions into a bowl and cover with water. Sprinkle with the salt and leave for 1 hour, then drain through a colander but do not rinse, and put into a large saucepan.

2. Mix all the remaining ingredients and bring slowly to the boil.

3. Pour the boiling mixture over the vegetables and leave to stand for 1 hour.

4. Bring everything very slowly to the boil, cover, and simmer gently for 10 minutes, stirring very gently from time to time, but being careful not to break up the courgettes.

5. Pot into sterilised jars.

Cucumbers - *concombre*

Another thing that grows easily is cucumber. Like everything else you really need more than one plant, as it helps with pollination, depending on the type of cucumber. The only problem is that we don't eat a lot of cucumbers. You might ask, in that case why don't you just buy one when you need it? The reason is that I only like cucumber when it is very fresh – on the day it is picked. Something happens to cucumber as it ages that gives it a smell/flavour I really don't like. For me the way to ruin a good gin and tonic is to put cucumber in it, especially a cucumber that has been sitting on a supermarket shelf for a day or so, but my children love cucumber and can chomp away on great chunks of it. Two ways of using up excess of cucumbers are cucumber pickle and an eastern European cucumber salad which is very elegant.

Cucumber Salad

Ingredients

- 1 cucumber
- 1 tbsp salt
- 150ml white wine or cider vinegar
- 1 tbsp sugar
- Chopped parley

Method

1. Slice the cucumber thinly using a mandolin. Layer in a colander with salt and leave to drain for an hour or two. Then layer on a clean tea towel and dry them with another tea towel laid on top. They don't need to be washed to get

rid of the salt. I then arrange the slices overlapping in a circle around a dinner plate ending in the middle. Mix the sugar and vinegar, sprinkle over the cucumber and then scatter the chopped parsley.

2. This a great salad to take to a BBQ. In summer, when there are a lot of strawberries around you can slice some strawberries and interleave them with the cucumber slices – these are particularly good with freshly ground black pepper.

Cucumber pickle

Another way to use up cucumbers is to pickle them. This cucumber pickle never lasts long in our house and is very easy to make.

Ingredients

- 3 large cucumbers thinly sliced
- 3 large onions (preferably red) thinly sliced
- 50g salt

- 500ml white wine or cider vinegar
- 150g soft brown sugar
- ½ tsp ground cloves (or some whole ones)
- ½ tsp ground turmeric
- ½ tsp fennel seeds
- 1 tbsp mustard seeds
- 4 or 5 x 450g sterilised jars

Method

1. In a large colander layer cucumbers and onions with the salt. Cover with a plate and a heavy weight and leave to drain for 3 or 4 hours, then pour off and squeeze out the excess liquid using a couple of clean tea-towels.

2. Mix the remaining ingredients in a large saucepan and stir over a medium heat until the sugar dissolves.

3. Add the drained cucumbers and onions, bring to the boil and simmer uncovered for about a minute.

4. Spoon the cucumber and onions into the sterilised jar with a draining spoon.

5. Return the vinegar mixture to the heat and boil rapidly for 5 – 10 minutes to reduce then top up the jars with the vinegar mixture.

6. Ideally store for a month before using, but its fine straight away. Great served with cold meats and cheese.

Garlic – '*Ail*'

Growing garlic in France is straightforward. They say it should be planted by St Catherine's day (25th November). However, there are many varieties of garlic and some are better planted in the spring. The main thing is that garlic needs a couple of months of cold weather, below 10C, to form cloves. So, if you don't want small cloves, but just one big clove, plant in spring!

Garlic scrapes are curly tendrils of greenery that come up from hard necked garlic plants terminating in something that looks like a bud. Cutting garlic scrapes is something to do as soon as they curl over because they soon become woody and lose their flavour. Cutting the garlic scrapes allows it to put its energy into the underground growth. Scrapes are superb steamed as a vegetable, stir fried or stirred into scrambled eggs.

Later, once the foliage starts to fade and go yellow, lift the bulbs with a fork to avoid damage. Also, avoid delay as the bulbs open up and store less well if left too long.

Dry them off thoroughly in a single layer in the sun, protected from rain, take care to avoid excessive (>30°C) heat by ventilating well. Expect drying to take two to four weeks depending on the weather. Once foliage is no longer moist cut off stalks and store the bulbs in a dry place at 5-10°C where further drying will take place. Soft-neck varieties of garlic can be braided, otherwise store in nets, in a cool, dry dark place.

The 'best' garlic, apparently, for French chefs is the Lautrec pink garlic. Due to the extended drying time (a minimum of 15 days), it is well-suited to long-term storage. It is sold with extended, rigid floral stems that produce clusters of garlic (called '*manouilles*') as it is a hard neck variety, so can't be plaited.

Aillet

'*Aillet*' is a young garlic plant. The head is not yet formed, it looks like a young, slightly purple leek. To eat it, remove the green parts of the top and the first skin. It brings a little freshness to dishes without the strong flavour of garlic.

La fête de l'aillet

In south-west France, on May the First (Labour Day), which in France is always a bank holiday, or feast day, you will find signs outside restaurants for young garlic omelettes - *l'omelette à l'aillet*. They also make some very big omelettes – for example in Bergerac the '*Jeune Chambre Economique de Bergerac*' make an '*aillet*' omelette with well over 2000 eggs each year

These *aillet* omelettes, by tradition are accompanied with a sweet wine such as Monbazillac.

The story goes that by consuming an *aillet* omelette on 1st May, fevers will be kept at bay for a year. It is also said that a sprig of *aillet* in hand on 1st of May, means money in the pocket all year.

Clear Garlic Soup

This soup clears the head - great if you've got a cold on the way.

Ingredients:

- 30g dried mushrooms soaked in 250 ml boiling water (add extra fresh mushrooms if available)
- 1 tbsp olive oil
- 1 onion, finely chopped
- A thumb sized piece of ginger, peeled and grated
- 1 whole garlic bulb, peeled (break the cloves up into a jar and shake hard, most of the skins will come off)
- 1 litre stock, can be made from a cube or something similar
- Juice 1 lemon
- Sea salt and freshly ground black pepper to taste

Method:

1. Heat the oil in a heavy-based pan. Add the onion and ginger then crush in all the garlic cloves. Fry gently until softened and aromatic.

2. Add the mushrooms and their water to the pan, plus any fresh mushrooms, then stir in the stock and the lemon juice.

3. Season then gently simmer with the lid on for at least 2 hours.

Tourain – the soup of the Perigord

Whilst living in the Perigord, I have frequently had Tourain soup in a variety of restaurants. It is the garlic soup of the area, but not always to my taste. The recipe below was given to me by my friend Marie Lachèze, and is the best one I've come across.

Ingredients

- 1 – 1.5 heads garlic, peeled and roughly chopped
- 2 litres water
- Stock made from 3 – 4 stock cubes – chicken or vegetarian
- 3 – 4 egg separated
- Cornflour (Maizena)

Method

1. Bring the 2 litres of water to the boil with the stock cubes, add the garlic

2. Cook until the garlic has almost entirely dissolved. There will always be tougher bits floating around but this doesn't matter. Check seasoning

3. Take 3 – 4 egg yolks, and when the liquid has cooled, beat into the soup.

4. Heat gently to thicken, BUT DO NOT BOIL – or it will curdle. This gives a lightly thickened soup

5. Strain

6. At this point for a creamier soup, add a good tablespoon of cornflour and heat until the soup has thickened.

Notes:

7. You can add more or less garlic to taste.

8. Local recipes often add the egg white as well as the yolk, this results in little white flecks which you may or may not, like.

9. If the soup accidentally curdles, adding the cornflour will smooth it out.

Hemerocallis – Day Lilies

Day lilies, the ordinary orange variety, grow like a weed here, but do have some saving graces. They are attractive to look at when in flower in early summer, and their dried buds are used in Chinese cooking and they make an exciting looking hors d'oeuvre stuffed with a flavoured ricotta cheese. They are also really invasive, and some kinds are poisonous to cats, although mine never had a problem with them.

Stuffed Day Lilies

To make a dish of stuffed day lilies, pick your daylilies early in the morning on the day you are going to use them (they won't keep overnight – hence the common name.)

Gently pull out the stamens.

Mix a small tub of ricotta or cream cheese, such as Philadelphia with lemon zest and nutmeg.

Stuff the mixture into the centre of the flowers, easiest using a piping bag.

Top with blue borage flowers, or other edible flowers

Figs 'figues'

Figs grow well in the Périgord. There are lots of varieties to choose from, but you may have just the rather small greenish native fig – as we do. The dark red "Rouge de Bordeaux" are said to be one of the best of all varieties.

Ours grow on top of a south facing slope in rather poor soil. Bear in mind that figs can get very big and grow rampantly. It is a good idea to restrict their root growth for several reasons – to protect your foundations for one – but also to grow fruit rather than leaves. A large hole lined with paving stones and half filled with rubble at the bottom should do the trick.

Fig trees can produce two different types of fruits: The breba fruits are the ones produced on over-wintered wood. Unfortunately, the breba crops are often barely edible, and often get frosted off in any case, so the advice is often to prune off the breba figs so that all growth flows into the main crop. The main fig crop develops on the current year's shoot growth and ripens in late summer or early autumn.

Again, the big issue is that to do with all the fruit. One solution is to make Fig and Apple chutney which is very traditional in the south-west, especially to accompany 'foie gras', but equally good with cheese and cold meat. When the figs ripen there is normally a glut of apples too, so, make some fig and apple chutney.

Fig & Apple Chutney

This chutney is traditional in the south-west of France and is particularly good with *foie-gras*, and makes a great accompaniment to cold meat, cheese and curry

Ingredients

- 1kg figs

- 250g brown sugar (whatever you can get)

- 300ml cider vinegar

- 250g chopped onions

- 250g chopped apples, dried cranberries, prunes or other fruit

- 1 tsp salt

- 1 tsp allspice

- ½ tsp black pepper

- 3 cloves garlic

- 4cm piece fresh ginger grated

- 1 tsp crush coriander seeds

- 1 fresh chilli (without seeds unless you like the heat)

Method

1. Chop the figs roughly, place in a large stainless (non-reactive) steel pan together with all the other ingredients except the sugar.

2. Bring to the boil and simmer until the onions and fruit are soft (about 30 minutes).

3. Stir in the sugar and bring back to the boil. Reduce heat and simmer until thick enough to see the bottom of the pan when a wooden spoon is pulled through it. This could take 10 – 15 minutes.

4. When thick, put into warm sterilised jars and seal. It's probably best left in a dark place before eating, but it is delicious straightaway.

It is so delicious that if you have enough figs it is worth making a double quantity. It will soon disappear.

Confiture de Figue

My delightful neighbour gave me the following recipe for '*Confiture de Figue*' which I reproduce, envelope and all. It will help your French:

This recipe makes a wonderful gift. It isn't difficult although it doesn't use up many figs.

Confiture de figues.

Pour 1 kg de fruits =

    1 kg de sucre cristallisé
    1 gousse de vanille
    1 zeste de citron
    2 décilitres d'eau (environ)

- Choisir des figues bien mûres, les laisser entières, les piquer avec une aiguille à tricoter.
- les laisser blanchir 5 minutes à l'eau bouillante. Egoutter.
- dans l'eau où les figues ont blanchi, faire fondre et cuire 1/4 d'heure leur poids en sucre avec 1 gousse de vanille et le zeste d'un citron.
- Ajouter les figues et laisser cuire une vingtaine de minutes.
- Mettre en pot après avoir écumé.

You can also dry figs in the sun or in a dehydrator, rather like tomatoes. These can be eaten later in the year, chopped in breakfast cereal or used to make fig rolls

Fig Rolls

Ingredients

- 125g softened butter

- 75g icing sugar (preferable unrefined golden) plus extra for dusting

- 1 tsp vanilla extract

- 1 large egg yolk

- 200g plain flour *'farine fluide'* plus a little extra for dusting

- 250g soft semi-dried figs, or double if using fresh figs

- Finely grated zest and juice 1 lemon

- Splash port or sherry

- Pinch of ground mixed spice (this is peculiarly English – use *'quatre-épices'* in France for similar result)

Method

Make the fig paste

Finely chop figs and heat gently with lemon juice port and spice until very soft then blend to a smooth paste. If you are using figs from the garden, they will be fresh rather than semi-dried, so you will need somewhat more than 250g. The aim is to destalk, chop and cook into a paste, adjust other ingredients accordingly. What you don't use this time refrigerate/freeze and use for a future batch of fig rolls.

Make the pastry

1. Beat butter, icing sugar and vanilla in a food processor until light pale and creamy,

2. Beat in the egg yolk, incorporating it fully

3. Add flour and bring together into a soft dough, adding more flour if needed.

4. Wrap the dough in cling film and put in the fridge for 30 minutes to relax.

Make the fig rolls

1. Preheat oven to 150°C

2. Turn the dough out onto a floured work surface and roll out into a rectangle 20 x 30cm

3. Cut in half lengthwise

4. Spoon the fig mixture down the centre of the pastry lengths, making sure it is distributed evenly

5. Fold the dough over the filling and gently roll so the join is on the underside and the top is smooth.

6. Cut each roll into 8 pieces

7. Gently indent the tops with a fork

8. Place the rolls onto a baking sheet and chill for half an hour

9. Bake for 30 -40 minutes until pale golden and set

10. Cool completely and dust with icing sugar

Nuts - 'Noix'

Simply translated 'nut' is 'noix', but in France 'noix' means
Walnut. The walnut is extremely important across France, and
especially in the Perigord.

Walnuts

In season, walnuts can be bought fresh or what is known as 'wet',
but most are sold as dry in their shells or even as kernels in packets.
The heat in a kitchen can cause the fat in your walnuts to change
structure, and the nut itself can become rancid, so it is best to keep
them fresh in the freezer or fridge and in an airtight package. Nut oil is
very fragrant but must be used cold (and kept cool because it quickly
goes rancid).

In the tenth century, the peasants paid their debts in walnuts. Nut
oil was considered as precious as gold. It was walnut oil that first
contributed to the fortune of the region. It was used to illuminate the

humble hovels and the most majestic cathedrals, and three-quarters of the peasants used it for cooking. In the Perigord walnuts have even been found in the dwellings of Cro-Magnon man.

Walnuts do not like the frost, and in years of hard frosts production has been badly affected. To combat this in the 1950's the Franquette variety was introduced in new '*noyeraies*' as it flowers later than some of the other varieties.

It is said that until the end of the 19th century, you could divide France into 3. In the north there was the France which cooked with butter, the Mediterranean regions where they cooked with olive oil and the south-west extending from the Limousin to the Pyrenees, where they cooked with walnut oil.

Even today in the south-west walnuts are everywhere, along the roadsides and in orchards. They even sell special devices to roll across the ground – a bit like a rugby ball made of wires – to harvest walnuts, which otherwise is a back-breaking job.

Vin de Noix

In the Périgord, young walnuts and leaves are collected to make '*Vin De Noix*'. Traditionally collection is done on St John's Day (June 24) and no later than Bastille Day (July 14th). The recipe below uses leaves.

Ingredients

- 500g walnut tree leaves
- 1 litre '*eau-de-vie*' (You can find this the supermarket)
- 4 litres semi-dry white wine
- 1kg castor sugar '*sucre en poudre*'
- 4 cloves
- 1-piece cinnamon

- Peel of half an orange

Method

1. Clean the leaves, without washing

2. Place them in a large demi-john with the '*eau-de-vie*'

3. Leave to soak for 2 days

4. Add remaining ingredients

5. Leave to rest for at least 20 days

6. Strain and pour into bottles

7. Drink over ice

Vin de Noix using the nuts

There are many recipes for making *Vin de Noix* with walnuts. They must be picked before the shells harden (end of June). Cut the walnuts into 4 or crush with a hammer and leave to macerate in either *eau-de-vie*, or other spirit such as Armagnac, grappa or vodka. Use 24 nuts to 1 litre of alcohol and half a kilo of sugar. Shake for a few days until the sugar has dissolved, leave for 3 months and filter into clean bottles, leave for at least 3 more months before serving as a *digestif*.

Some recipes call for brown sugar, others use additional flavourings such a juniper berries, vanilla pods, cinnamon sticks, cloves stuck in oranges, and others add red wine. (Warning, careful how much you drink – it can have a laxative effect.)

Pickled Walnuts

Pickled Walnuts are a peculiarly English delight and you are very unlikely to find any in France, but if you have a walnut tree, or access to one, they are not difficult to make and are good Christmas presents.

Method

1. Walnuts must be picked very young, before the shell forms inside. Once that has happened, they will be unpleasant to eat both because of the shell and because they will be bitter. The time to pick them is mid/late June – with some variation across the country and the season/variety. You must be able to push a needle/skewer through them easily.

2. Make a brine (100g salt to 1 litre of water), top and tail the walnuts and prick the skins all over and soak in brine for a week. Drain and soak in fresh brine for another week. Drain and spread out in the sun to dry for a couple of days or until they are completely black.

3. Pack into jars and cover with spiced vinegar

   - You can buy spiced vinegar in the UK or make your own. If in the UK, you will probably use malt vinegar. In France there is a wide range of vinegars you can choose from, but not malt vinegar. I would use cider vinegar, but you can use any you can get hold of, but perhaps not the kind you would use for cleaning.

     To 1 litre of vinegar add pickling spice: 2-star anise, 1 cinnamon stick, 5 cloves, 1 tsp of peppercorns, 1 small chilli and a small piece of root ginger, bay leaf.

   - Then how much sugar you add depends on how sweet you like your pickled walnuts – anything from 100g – 500g, as brown as you can find.

   - Dissolve the sugar in the vinegar, add the spices and bring to the boil for 5 minutes.

4. Cool the vinegar and pour over the walnuts.

They should be ready for the following Christmas, when they are traditionally eaten. They are brilliant with bread and cheese or cold meats.

Walnut Butter

If you have an excess of walnuts in the garden, one simple thing to make, which costs a lot to buy, is walnut butter – like peanut butter – only better. You can use the nuts as they are or bake them in the oven for about 12 minutes at 150°C, until looking a bit oily on top and smelling fragrant. Don't do them too long or you will burn them.

Put the nuts into a food-processor and blitz until smooth and buttery, scraping down the sides from time to time. It can take 5 – 10 minutes. The roasted ones get smooth and oily more quickly.

You can season with salt, or honey or stevia for a sweetened version.

Walnut Fact:

One thing walnuts are known for is their ability to stain, indeed they are used traditionally to stain wood on old buildings, so do wear gloves and an apron if you are going to do anything with young unripe nuts. The stain is indelible. It is known as *'Brou de noix'* and can be purchased in most supermarkets.

Chestnuts – *'châtaigne'* – *'marron'*

When we first came here, I was confused by someone saying there are two kinds of chestnuts. It crossed my mind they may have been talking about chestnut and horse-chestnut, but I was wrong. There are two types of sweet chestnut. The *'châtaigne'* is correctly called the Spanish Chestnut and from each fruit, there will anything from one to five kernels, usually three. The *'marron'* is the American chestnut and it usually has a single larger kernel in each fruit, sometimes two. These are used for *'marron glace'*, crystallised chestnuts, which is a prized sweet treat in France. However, horse-chestnut trees are called *'Marronnier d'Inde'*. Everyone knows horse chestnuts are poisonous to eat, so you would not expect to find their conkers crystallised, but the naming convention in French is confusing. One of our favourite restaurants is called Les Marronniers, simply because their garden is shaded by a row of horse chestnut trees.

Some 25% of France is covered with sweet-chestnut forests from the north to the south. Chestnuts were, for hundreds of years, the primary food of the French peasantry; it kept them alive through the winters because chestnut flour *'farine de châtaigne'* stored well.

Collecting and using chestnuts

Collecting chestnuts is a very prickly job. You need thick gloves, and if you can collect them without their spiny outer case (burr), so much the better. You can use one of those nut gatherers they use for walnuts, if you have one. If the burr is open, you can usually use the edge of your shoe and gloved hand to remove it. Chestnut woods are to be avoided as a place to take your dog or any other animal for a walk during the chestnut picking season.

Discard any with wormholes or other signs of damage. Worms are a major problem, and if you keep chestnuts in a bag for a few days, one wormy nut will affect most of the others. So, promptly store the chestnuts in air-tight containers and refrigerate or freeze. In the old days they use to smoke them to kill the worms. Chestnut farmers are meticulous about picking up all fallen debris every autumn to try and break the cycle.

Chestnuts are delicious roasted over a log fire, or can be used in stuffing, with vegetables, in soup or made into *'Marron glacé'*.

Okra

My liking for okra, (aka ladies' fingers or gumbo), is probably a reflection of growing up in Kenya. It is difficult to buy here, except in Grand Frais, so hence my need to grow it myself. It does better here than in the UK as it really does like heat and a lot of sunshine.

Unfortunately, the deer like it even more than I do, so it can be frustrating. It has very beautiful flowers, and I use it a lot in curry – particularly a dry curry where you don't get the 'slime' which puts a lot people off.

Just fry a pinch of fenugreek seeds and half a teaspoonful each of cumin and mustard seeds in a little oil, add 350g of okra sliced into 1cm pieces, add half a teaspoon each of ground coriander, chilli and turmeric and a pinch of asafoetida, cook gently until the mixture is dry, at the end add 3 cloves of garlic crushed with half a teaspoon of salt.

Peas

Peas have been a big disappointment to me here in France. In England I used to buy frozen peas, probably Birds Eye peas. They were always good, and I never felt the need to grow my own. On the few occasions I bought some fresh on a market I found them to be inferior, not so sweet, starchier, so the frozen ones lived up to their advertisement: "frozen garden peas are picked fresh and frozen within hours".

On arrival in France I bought my first packet of frozen peas. They were not great, too starchy, not frozen fresh enough. This coincided with a trip to the vet with one of the cats. He was feeling around the cat's neck, and I asked what he was looking for. His answer was: "English peas", which really puzzled me. The next day at my French class I asked the teacher, what he'd meant by "English peas", and she turned around and said, "Everyone knows that English peas are round and hard"! Of course, I protested and said that English peas are better than anything I had found in France. When I admitted that all I'd tried were frozen, she said with some distain, that "no self-respecting French person would ever eat frozen peas, and that they were only stocked by the supermarkets for the British". She then asked me how to cook them! Turns out that the French still think we eat marrowfat peas in England – not something I've ever tried but were apparently a bit of a war-time speciality, dried and brought back to life by soaking in water. After that I tried buying some fresh off the market, but like the English ones they had hung around for too long. This might well explain why the French are so fond of pureed peas, in fact pureed vegetables in general.

So, since then I've grown a crop or two of peas each year, just to pick and freeze. OK, a fair few get eaten out in the potager – you can't get fresher than that. I take great care not to leave them too long before picking, or indeed after picking before blanching and freezing.

I've discovered on our hot dry plot that I get a better crop from peas sown before Christmas. Spring sown ones do not like the heat we often experience in February, March and April. I've grown many varieties from tiny Provencal petit pois to standard Kelvedon Wonder. Now I only grow the very tall old fashion ones like Lord Leicester and Carter's Telephone peas.

Plums and Greengages

There are many varieties of plums '*prune/pruneaux*' sold in France. The most famous are the dried '*Pruneaux d'Agen*'. There are also the small yellow/pink '*Mirabelle*' and the purple plums (which the French call '*la quetsche*') to '*Reines-Claudes*' which are greengages. My impression is that '*mirabelles*' are considered inferior, but I use them to make jams and jellies and fruit juice.

Mirabelle Juice

When a '*mirabelle*' tree starts to produce fruit, it will produce an enormous amount, and the big issue is what to do with it all. Obviously, you can collect them and try to sell them, give them away, or make jam '*confiture*' or jelly, or just leave them on the ground for the wasps. I hate waste, so I make juice, which I freeze and drink over the year instead of orange or apple juice.

To make Mirabelle juice

1. Collect up to 3kg of good fruit

2. Wash and get rid of any bad bits, leaves or other debris

3. Put in a large pan, possibly used for jam making with maybe a tablespoon of water to stop any burning initially.

4. Put a lid on the pan on and turn up to a relatively high heat,

5. After a few minutes the juices will start to run

6. After 10 to 15 minutes they will all have cooked down into a mush. At this point turn off the heat.

7. Suspend a large jelly strainer/ muslin bag/ pillowcase over a large bowl and tip the contents of the pan into it.

8. Leave to strain overnight.

9. The juice thus collected can be used to make jelly (don't squeeze the bag if you want the jelly to be clear), or can be frozen in plastic boxes, for later use or to drink (no sugar needed).

To us the other wonderful plum, not normally seen on the markets is Prunus cerasifera or Myrobalan plum. This purple leaf plum grows on a medium-sized deciduous tree. It is planted most often because of its deep reddish-purple leaves and pale pink flowers which are among the first to appear in spring. It has small, almost invisible cherry plums, which the birds love, and which we ignored for a few years until a Dutch neighbour told us they make the best plum jam, and boy was he right! Far better than the jam from 'mirabelles'.

Red plum jam

Ingredients

- 1.5kg Red Plums, halved and stoned (or you can use a cherry stoner)

- 400ml water

- 1.25kg *Sucre Cristal* (or jam sugar with added pectin, or 1 lemon or you could use a sachet of Vitpris)

Method

1. Put the plums in a large preserving pan. Bring to the boil and simmer gently for 15 -20 mins or until the plum skins are soft (It is important that they are soft before the sugar is added, or the skins will be hard)

2. Add sugar, bring to the boil and boil rapidly for about 10 mins or until setting point is reached. Note the lemon or Vitpris helps to shorten the cooking time. Without either I often have to boil them for up to 30 minutes. Setting point is reached when the mixture reaches 104.5°C

3. Remove any scum (or a lump of butter will disperse this). Pour into cooled, sterilised jars. Seal and label.

My next recipe can be made with small tart red plums or use sloes from the hedgerow. The recipe is the similar for both.

Damson Gin - Sloe Gin

Ingredients:

- 500g sloes (frosted, pricked or dumped in the freezer overnight)

- 300g sugar

- 600ml gin – I use the cheapest from the supermarket for this

Method:

1. Combine sloes (or damsons/plums) in a large jar with sugar and gin.

2. Give it a good shake to mix up the contents,

3. Shake daily for the next week, there after once a week for the next 8 – 10 weeks.

4. Strain and bottle.

It should be ready to drink by Christmas.

Use the fruit, stones removed, at the base of Boxing Day trifle, or with ice-cream. The remaining fruit will store well in the freezer.

Potatoes

Potatoes tend to be rather sweet in France (not to be confused with sweet potatoes), and are not deeply savoury like Maris Piper, or King Edwards used especially for roasting in the UK.

In the supermarket potatoes are sold for '*Frites*' (Chips/French fries or is that Belgian fries?), '*four*' (oven), '*salade*' or for steaming, and mostly are marked with their variety name as well.

People often suggest that Agata are a good substitute for Maris Piper. But they are just not the same – not as crispy on the outside nor as fluffy on the inside. Currently two other varieties are being recommended – Sirco and Binjt but the local Fish & Chip van remains faithful to Maris Piper which are specially imported.

Storing potatoes – roast potatoes

If you grow potatoes in your potager and have perhaps quite a few that are not perfect for storing, peel them, get rid of any bad bits, cut them to size for roasting and par boil them - less than 7 minutes - and freeze them in portions. When you are doing a roast during the winter, they are a real time saver. Just get them out of the freezer, drop them into hot fat/oil and they will roast brilliantly straight from frozen.

If you have any fat left over from a can of *Confit de Canard*, then use this for roasting your potatoes.

Potato and pea samosas

Ingredients

- 600g potatoes, peeled, boiled until soft and crushed into large lumps
- 60g fresh or frozen peas
- 1 small onion chopped
- packet of 'Brick' pastry
- 3 tbsp vegetable oil
- ½ tsp mustard seeds
- 1 tsp finely grated ginger
- 1 tbsp ground coriander
- 1 tsp ground cumin
- ¼ tsp red chilli powder
- 1 tsp garam masala
- 1-2 tsp dried amchoor, (or, juice of 1/2 a lemon)
- salt, to taste
- 4 tbsp chopped fresh coriander leaves
- 5 tbsp melted butter, for brushing

Preparation method

1. Heat the oil in a non-stick pan and fry the mustard seeds for about ten seconds, or until they begin to splutter.

2. Add the onion and ginger and cook for 2-3 minutes over a high heat. Add the peas, stir well and add the spices, salt and a splash of water or the lemon juice if using. Cook for 1-2 minutes, then add the potatoes and coriander and cook for 2-3 minutes. Taste and adjust the seasoning.

3. Preheat the oven to 200C/400F/Gas 6.

4. Take the 'Brick' pastry out if the packet and cut the circles in half so you end up with 20 half circles. Peel the paper off one half circle and fold so that the edge of the circle meets the cut middle line and brush with melted butter. Put a teaspoonful of mixture near one end and fold into a triangle shape and repeat the fold several times along the length of the pastry. Brush again with the butter and place on an oven tray ready for baking.

5. Bake in the centre of the oven for 30-35 minutes, or until golden and crisp, turning halfway through the cooking time.

Purple Sprouting Broccoli

This is a vegetable I've never come across in France, and yet it is easy to grow and delicious steamed for about 5 minutes or made into cream of broccoli soup. In my garden it arrives at the same time as the asparagus.

It is the only brassica I now grow because it grows over the winter, flowering in the spring, and so does not compete with the shield bugs that conspire to eat all my summer cabbages, other greens, and coriander. They (pictured right) are confusingly like the gendarme beetles (with the two eyes marking on the left) that do no harm.

Quinces – 'coing'

The French for quince (Cydonia) is 'le coing', the tree being 'le cognassier'. We have two varieties, one pear shaped the other more apple shaped, in both cases they are a lot larger than an apple. They both have exquisitely beautiful pale pink flowers in spring. The

problem we have is that they both get brown patches on the fruit, and once that happens the whole fruit is destroyed within a day. The main cause seems to be damage from codling moths.

We don't do much about it, because even with a very reduced harvest, we still have far more than we know what to do with. That said, we need to use what fruit we get very rapidly and other than the odd crumble or baking a few slices around a piece of roast pork, the majority get made into quince jelly. People are often happy to receive a jar of quince jelly but not many are interested in the fresh fruit as it is practically inedible raw.

Membrillo – quince cheese - 'pâte de coing'

Start by wiping your quinces with a cloth to remove their down.

Wash them carefully then cut them into about 6 chunks, discarding any bad parts, but keeping seeds and skin. Most of the pectin is in the seeds.

Weigh them, and for each 1kg of quinces add 1 litre of water.

Cook quinces over medium heat until soft. This can take 20 - 40 minutes.

The next stage separates the juice from the pulp. The juice is used to make a beautiful clear jelly. The pulp is used to make membrillo (as it's known is Spain), quince cheese or *'pâte de coing'* as it is known in France

I use a large jelly bag to strain the juice off the fruit pulp. Ideally leave to strain overnight. Don't be tempted to squeeze the bag to maximize the juice if you want the result to be sparkling clear.

Preparation and cooking of the quince pulp

Go through the cooked quince pulp and remove the core (hard part and seeds). You can push what is left through a chinois or use a vegetable mill to separate the skin from the pulp.

Weigh the pureed quince and add it to its own weight in sugar.

Put everything in a jam pan and bring to the boil, stirring all the time. Take care, use a long wooden spoon, cover your hand with a tea towel and stand back because it can get rather like a volcano and quite explosive. It is cooked when a spatula/spoon is scraped on the bottom of the pot and you can see the bottom before the two sides of puree meet again.

Drying quince puree

Pour the thickened puree into a container large enough to accommodate it (a baking tray for example, or a shallow dish) cover with a clean cloth and let it dry for at least 3 days.

This time will be longer according to the thickness of the puree (i.e. the depth of your dish), and the ambient temperature. The quince puree needs a dry and airy atmosphere.

Check the solidification from time to time by touching it, when the puree resists the pressure of your finger and is not tacky; it is ready.

Cut into cubes and roll (or not) in caster sugar.

Preservation of quince cheese

Quince cheese, better known as membrillo[9] can be preserved for a very long time. I wrap it in baking paper, which I put in the fridge. I keep my membrillo almost from one year to the next. If you do roll it in sugar only do so shortly before serving, otherwise it tends to become liquid.

Quince jelly

Pour the strained juice (see above) into a jam pan and add its weight in sugar and 100ml of cider vinegar per kg of sugar. Put back on the heat and boil.

After about 10 minutes test for set (104.5C) or with the saucer test: drop a drop of jelly on a saucer and hold the saucer vertically. If the drop 'slips', it is not cooked enough, if it freezes, stop cooking immediately. The longer it cooks, the darker the jelly will become.

Potting quince jelly

Pour your jelly into airtight sterilised jars.

---

[9] I use the name 'membrillo' which is the Spanish name for quince cheese or 'pâte de coing', as it is much more widely sold there and eaten for breakfast with Manchego cheese, and I have rarely see it for sale in the UK or in France.

Quince jelly is very good on toast as well as with cold meat, such as lamb, instead of red currant jelly. It is also excellent in the base of a frangipani tart, and I use it for glazing tarts, such as Normandy apple tarts - or anything else that needs glazing.

Japanese Quinces - Chaenomelese

In addition to the quince trees we have half a dozen Japanese quince (chaenomelese – '*cognassier du Japon*') shrubs. These too are very pretty in flower early in the year. There are many colours, orange and red being the most common, but they also exist in white and apricot colours.

Japanese Quince Jelly

Normally Japanese quinces are grown for the flowers and their hedge making ability. However, they also bear quinces in the autumn, which, in themselves are inedible, but cooked in the same way as standard quinces make wonderful quince jelly, almost indistinguishable from the real thing.

I use these for making jelly, and in many ways its easier than real quince because they are less affected by codling moth and they hang around on the bushes for months. However, I've never tried to make membrillo with them.

Radishes

The standard summer radish is a popular vegetable in France. It is easy to grow, and in spring easy to find in supermarkets and markets.

Radishes with butter

You see radishes on the menu for school canteens served up in a way I've never seen in the UK. In France radishes are served with butter. Either a pat of butter on the side of the plate, or the radish is split lengthwise with butter spread down the centre. Either way there is also salt to dip into on the plate. Absolutely delicious! We've also found that a handful of radishes fresh from the potager with some salt an excellent *apéro* to go with a glass of wine – perhaps a bit healthier than a bowl of crisps or '*chips*' as they are known in France.

Radish tops

Another thing we discovered here is that the green tops of the radishes make excellent greens, steamed, in place of other more usual greens with a meal. They also make great soup, pesto and can be used where you might otherwise use say spinach, in quiche, salad and so on. Just make sure you wash them well, especially if bought as they can be very sandy.

Sage

Butter fried Sage on Pasta

In our sunny south facing garden we grow a lot of sage; several variegated varieties as well as culinary ones. They all grow and flower well. The one I grow for cooking purposes has very large leaves, and besides using them in stuffing we fry them in butter to have on pasta. It's such a simple meal to boil up some pasta and pour over the browned butter and sage leaves, that it is hard to believe what a satisfying, and economical meal this can be. But it is!

Another tasty way of eating sage leaves it to dip them in batter, deep

fry and dish up with apéros.

Sage Fritters

Ingredients

- 4 tbs heaped of plain flour – farine fluide
- 50ml beer
- 100ml water
- Salt and pepper to taste
- 30 – 40 sage leaves
- Olive oil or grape seed oil (*Huile de Pépins de Raisin*)

Method

1. Make the batter in a bowl slowly adding beer and water to the dry ingredients avoiding lumps. Rest in the fridge for half an hour to chill.

2. Using a wide based pot or pan heat your oil until shimmering. Dip the leaves into the batter shaking of the excess, and lay the leaves in the hot oil, well-spaced apart, fry until golden. Do in batches so that they don't stick together.

3. Remove the sage leaves from the oil, place onto the plate with a few sheets of paper towel to absorb the excess oil.

4. Sprinkle with salt and serve immediately

Sweet Potatoes

One of the biggest menaces in my potager when it comes to weeds is bind weed, part of the convolvulus family of plants like Morning Glory and related Ipomoeas. Since bind weed grows so well, I thought I'd give sweet potatoes (also part of the Ipomoea family) a go too. I bought one from the supermarket, the kind with a red skin and a white inside (a preference reflecting my childhood in Kenya), kept part of it over winter in the shed, and then when spring came planted out the shoots which sprung for the part I'd kept. They were rampant! Pretty with pale lilac flowers reflecting the shape of their cousins. I dug up more than a barrow load in the autumn after the first frosts had blackened the tops. More than we could ever eat.

Keeping Sweet Potatoes

They must be cured before eating by leaving in a warm humid place for a few weeks, the curing enhances their sweetness and heals any wounds, which means they will then store well over most of the winter.

Sweetcorn – 'maïs doux'

Most of the maize you see growing in fields in France is intended for either animal feed or oil production and is not suitable for human consumption. Growing your own specially bred varieties, there is nothing to beat them, cooked the moment you pick them. They say you should put the pot onto boil whilst you go into the garden to pick them and cook them immediately. There is no doubt that buying them from the supermarket and cooking them a day or two later does not match up. By then all the sugars have converted into starch.

I no longer grow sweet corn because I picked a cob one day and inside it was like Frankenstein corn. I posted a picture of it on Facebook (Gardeners Together in France), and was told it was corn smut and should be burnt.

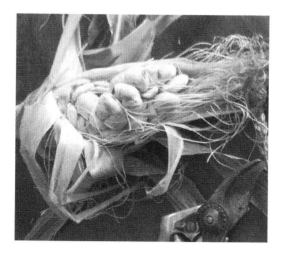

Huitlacoche

I looked it up on Google and apparently in Mexico they call corn-smut 'huitlacoche' or Mexican truffle and earn a fortune from it as the high-end restaurants like to cook it for their customers. A friend and I cooked some up in a sort of stir fry and had it for lunch - it tastes a bit like mushrooms, but it wasn't exciting enough for me to carry on growing it.

After that, on my walks, I noticed that a lot of maize '*maïs*' the farmers were growing was also affected.

I've given up growing sweetcorn because of the corn smut infection. Apparently, it takes 8 years for the fungus spores to disappear from the soil, and with surrounding farms infected, it will take even longer.

Tomatoes

Tomatoes are easily grown, and a wide selection is available at the many plant markets that pop up in spring, and even the cut price supermarkets carry sets of heritage varieties. Personally, I like to grow half a dozen different varieties, and sow, under cover, maybe 5 seeds of each early each year. This means I've usually have quite a few to give away, and still have far too many, which means of course, deciding what to do with them.

Blight

The problem for most people growing tomatoes is that both early and late blight can strike. Apparently, blight needs 2 consecutive days, each with a minimum of 11 hours when the relative humidity is 89 percent or more and the minimum temperature is 10°C. These conditions are easily found in south 'Dordogneshire'!

What can you do about blight?

Blight resistant varieties are available, but my experience is that they are not totally blight free. Last year I tried a new variety called 'Honeymoon'. Of all the 'blight resistant' varieties I've tried they did a pretty good job of keeping blight at bay. 'Crimson Crush' was another one that performed reasonably well.

To avoid blight spray with Bordeaux mixture - *'bouillie bordelaise'*.

Practice good hygiene in the potager, and make sure plants are well spaced to ensure good air flow

Grow under cover, but then don't water with rainwater as I did once.

Last year I got early blight for the first time. I had got my plants ready early, then we had the wettest June on record, I'd mulched the tomato beds with wet green grass clippings, the tomatoes grew like mad, and voilà, I got blight. I pulled out some of the worst affected plants and disposed of them in black bin bags, and stripped some of the leaves off others, but had to leave them as I was embarking on an art course with a friend. So, my attitude was, 'blow it – they will just have to survive as best they can – there's no way I'm going to fuss around as I normally do and water them on a daily basis etc'.

From that point on the sun came out and we had one of the longest hottest driest summers we've experienced. The plants did not get watered at all. The miracle was, that the blight receded – you could see the silvery scars on the stems that were black originally, the plants produced a good crop of tomatoes and didn't seem to mind the lack of water at all. I was still picking tomatoes in November and didn't finally use up the last of them until after New Year. My feeling is that their roots followed the water down as the ground dried out, and if I had started to water them the roots would have stayed near the surface and they would have continued to need water all summer. So, the secret is, once established, do not water your tomatoes.

Blossom-end rot

This appears as black patches on the base of the tomatoes. It is often blamed on erratic watering and on lack of calcium. I try to remember to put crushed eggshells in the base of the planting hole to help ameliorate this. A French neighbour suggested that I use skimmed milk diluted with water to water a specimen that was affected, and lo and behold, the blossom end rot disappeared.

What to do with excess tomatoes

One of my favourite ways of using a tomato glut is to cut up tomatoes into even-size pieces and spread on a baking tray. Add about 4 cloves of garlic, a glug or two of olive oil and a few sprigs of thyme and a sprinkle of salt. Put into an oven at about 200°C for half an hour, or more. How long you leave it depends on how thick you want the result. I find half an hour is right to make superb tomato soup. Longer and more water evaporates so you end up with passata or tomato sauce.

Tomato Soup

The best tomatoes for soup are the big beefsteak varieties, such as Pink Brandy Wine, Honeymoon, Carbon, or Purple Cherokee, but any will do.

Once cooked, I like to blitz mine using a hand blender, briefly (too long and the pips will make the flavour bitter) and then pass them through a chinois. This is hard work, but the result is vastly superior to the version with all the fibre left in – on the other hand some folks like as much fibre as they can get in their diet.

So, for a classy meal, you can add cream or crème fraîche, dished up with freshly grated parmesan or a good strong cheddar and some fresh crusty baguette.

Passata

As for soup, the bigger varieties are best, especially 'Amish Paste' or other plum tomatoes which have few pips and lots of flesh. Again, the best sauce is made by making an effort to remove pips and skin. Freeze the result and use to make soup, sauce, bolognaise or other tomato-based recipes in the winter. You can add basil, oregano to flavour, adjust seasoning, adding sugar, salt and pepper, vinegar as the mood takes you.

Dried Tomatoes

Dried tomatoes are very popular with my family, as well as providing a means of long-term storage without the use of a freezer. You need three good days of sunshine to actually sun-dry them (as opposed to oven dry) or dehumidify them. You need to cover them to prevent flies and other bugs from crawling all over them.

You can speed up the process by putting tray of tomatoes on the dashboard of your car, which can get pretty hot sitting in the summer sun. Obviously, you can use a dehumidifier, but that does use electricity. You won't begrudge that, if after a couple of days, it gets cloudy and your half-dried tomatoes go mouldy. The dried tomatoes, if stored in a glass jar will keep for a year or even more in the fridge. If

you decide to keep them in olive oil, take care, or you could end up with botulism. Make sure any jar and jar lid you use is sterilised, that the tomatoes are really dry (but not crispy) before adding to oil. Don't add fresh herbs or garlic. Don't leave them sitting prettily on the window ledge in the sun. Dipping them in red wine vinegar immediately before adding the olive oil adds acidity and can help fight the bugs.

Tomato Balls

Another but more tedious, way of drying tomatoes is to cut out any bad bits and cook them up either in a large pot on top of the stove or in

the oven as described above. You need to get rid of as much liquid as you can either by long cooking or by pouring off the excess liquid (which is delicious by the way), then blending. Keep all the blended pips and skin and spread the paste onto a silicon sheet in the oven and leave to dry, either until you have 'leather' (which you can roll up for the kid's lunch boxes), or before that stage take spoonful's and roll into balls and leave the balls to dry in the sun for a few days, turning from time to time. Two oven trays full of tomatoes will end up as one large jar of tomato balls. They will keep in the fridge for a year or more.

I recommend always keeping dried tomatoes in the fridge because, it's dark, away from sunlight and bugs which multiply more slowly at low temperatures.

Tomato Juice

Some tomatoes are sweeter than others, depending on their ripeness and the variety of tomato. Use the ripest tomatoes you can. Added sugar will balance the natural acidity of the tomatoes. If you want your tomato juice a bit spicy you can add a shake or two of Tabasco sauce or some other chilli sauce.

Ingredients

- 1.5kg very ripe garden tomatoes, cored, roughly chopped
- 2 sticks chopped celery with leaves
- 1 small onion chopped
- 2 tbsp sugar (to taste)
- 1 tsp salt
- Pinch black pepper
- 6-8 drops chilli sauce

Method

1. Put all ingredients into a large non-reactive pot (use stainless steel, not aluminium).

2. Bring to a simmer and cook, uncovered, until mixture is completely soupy, about 25 minutes.

3. Force mixture through a sieve, chinois, or food mill. Cool completely.

4. Store covered and chilled.

5. Will last for about 1 week in the refrigerator.

6. Drink with or without Worcestershire Sauce, or a squeeze of lime.

Tomatillos

Tomatillos look rather like cape gooseberries with a papery lantern around them. They are also untidy plants sprawling along the ground. There is only so much you can do with these; I have used them in chutney but primarily I used them for making Salsa Verde.

Tomatillo Salsa Verde

This salsa is great used as a dip, and it's also delicious as a topping for rice or as an ingredient to lift the flavour of a lovely meaty taco.

Ingredients

- 400g tomatillos
- 2 mild green chillies
- 6 spring onions
- 1 large handful coriander
- 100ml water
- 1 tsp salt

Method

1. Remove the husks from the tomatillos and wash them to remove their natural sticky coating.

2. Halve them, removing the woody bit where stalk was.

3. Remove the seeds from the chillies and wash the spring onions and coriander carefully to remove any grit.

4. Put all the ingredients in the food processor, and whizz until you have a slightly chunky mixture. Chill before serving.

OTHER THINGS WHICH DRIVE YOU POTTY

Gardening

Gardening in France is not that different from gardening in the UK. At any moment in time there are, usually, only a few degrees centigrade difference between the two. Obviously, if you are gardening high up on a mountain, or in the very south the differences will be greater. The temperature difference between night and day is frequently greater because much of France has a "continental" climate as opposed to one ameliorated by being surrounded by the sea. You still need to worry about planting out dates, and when to bring plants in for the winter. In the UK old saying warned:

"Farmers fear unkindly May
Frost by night and hail by day."

In France gardening folks talk about the ice saints - *Les saints de glace*. There are five ice saints likely to become the coldest days, especially at night or in the morning

Saint George on April 23rd

Saint Marc on April 25

Saint Eutrope on April 30th

Saint Croix on May 2

Saint Jean Porte Latine on May 6 (The Saint who "closes the door to the cold")

They also point out that caution must also be exercised around several dates, which can be somewhat forgotten:

Saint Mamet on May 11

Saint Pancrace on May 12

Saint Gervais on May 13th, the most feared because the very last.

It's not unusual for people to visit the various plant fares in April, when the day time temperatures are in the middle to high 20's, buy a lot of bedding plants and vegetables, plant them out only to find them frosted in the first half of May[10]. Sometimes what you will see the French do is lean terracotta roof tiles against the tomato canes. During the day these warmup and hold heat. At night they create a 'tent' of two tiles leaning together over the small plants to keep them warm overnight.

The French are also very keen on gardening by phases of the moon, and almanacs to guide you in this process are published every year and can be found in agricultural and gardening shops as well as paper shops and supermarkets.

---

10   https://www.plantmaps.com/interactive-france-last-frost-date-map.php?fbclid=IwAR3-IeRBnPe6G0UKzkZGrW3hnfxqX_5SXGwVDR62LYl2-5qS72M5N8GJbhU

One thing we found very different here when we arrived was how seasonal everything was. If you didn't buy your geraniums, say, in April or May, you could forget it for the rest of the year. Now there are more garden centres along the lines of the ones in the UK so that it is possible to buy a plant for your lock-up holiday-home in, say, August.

Another thing we found different was the wide variety of potting composts and fertilisers. Maybe the UK has caught up in this respect. Before coming here, it wouldn't have occurred to me to buy potting compost especially for geraniums, or for citrus "*agrumes*" for example You can even buy vitamins for your strawberries or tomatoes, as well as special fertilisers '*engrais*' for almost anything you can think of – olives, boxwood, geraniums, etc. I used to buy ericaceous compost for the likes of rhododendrons, azaleas and camelias, otherwise used the 'normal' stuff. Which might have been a John Innes earth-based compost or something peat-based (or these days peat replacement).

One reader highly recommends Orgasyl compost. It is organic, with a root booster.

Pralin

When planting bare rooted plants such as roses, hedging plant or trees, it is considered important in France not to forget the operation of '*pralinage*'. Basically, this involves mixing up soil, water and compost (or decomposed manure) in a bucket to get a thick mud called '*pralin*'. Then, before you commit your plants to the hole you've dug for them, you dip them in the *pralin*. This operation contributes to the good recovery of the plant.

You can also buy a bucket of *pralin* from suppliers of garden and agricultural supplies.

Bordeaux Mixture – 'bouillie bordelaise'

Bordeaux mixture It is a combination of copper sulphate, lime and water and is frequently used to control many diseases include fungi, mildew, scab, blistering fruit and cankers on plants, vegetables and fruit trees in your garden. It is used as a spray.

It is authorized in organic 'bio' agriculture in France but not the UK.

How to use it?

Use between 10g and 20g per litre of water.

It is usually used at the end of winter to eliminate fungi that have overwintered in the vegetation. In the spring, it is recommended that you use it regularly, especially when the weather is hot and humid, as fungi and/or diseases tend to develop quickly.

For fruit trees, spray it on when the leaves fall from the trees. At the end of winter, repeat the treatment to protect wounds from fungi. When the dead leaves fall, pick them up before spraying.

In early spring, when the first buds appear, repeat your treatment again. The operation will need to be repeated 2, or even 3 times at 15-day intervals to be effective.

For tomatoes, potatoes or strawberries, treat from May onwards, with a spray of Bordeaux mixture every 15 days.

Because of the copper content, sprayed plants stain blue. This is very unsightly, so don't over-do it. You can buy 'Bouille Bordelaise non-colorée', which does not stain the plants or the walls supporting them, as much.

Savon noir – black soap

In France Savon Noir is very popular for both garden and household use. A popular brand 'Marius Fabre' is made from olive oil, so it is 100% natural and biodegradable. You can use it to rid your plants of sooty mould deposited on the leaves by aphids, which is not only unsightly but also suffocates the leaves. You can do this by making a mixture of water and black soap (5 tablespoons of black soap for 1 litre of water). Pour this mixture into a sprayer. Spray the leaves of your plants to protect them from aphids.

Savon noir also has many uses for cleaning surfaces in the house and oven, washing your pets and your own hair, cleaning things like leather, silver and copper, dishes and laundry. Personally, I find the smell of 'savon noir' quite pleasant but if you are using it in the house, rather than just in the garden, you can scent it with lemon oil, lavender oil, rosemary for example. There are many recipes on the internet.

Hornets

The 'European Hornet' (vespa crabro) is native to Europe and is protected in countries further north. It is normally peaceful and does not attack if you cross its path, and it plays a great job in the garden eating insects such as greenfly. The 'Asian Hornet' or *'Frelon Asiatique'* (vespa velutina) is a recent arrival and will attack in swarms if you get too close to its nest and it decimates the bee population, feeding the bees and their honey to its young. However, unlike the European hornet, the Asian hornet is not attracted by light at night; the whole colony stays in the nest and lets you enjoy your terrace, and, foraging away from the nest, it is not aggressive.

Risk to humans from this species is minimal except when and if, they consider their nest to be under threat. Otherwise they are more timid than the European Hornet and their sting is no worse than that of an ordinary wasp.

Until recently, the advice was to trap the queens of Asian Hornets early in the year to prevent breeding, but many other species also got trapped at the same time as it is difficult to make the traps selective enough. The laws surrounding destruction of their nests is constantly changing, so you should check with your *Mairie*, if you have a nest on your property. Currently there is a legal obligation on the property owner to have nests destroyed.

The colonies of the Asian Hornet live only for one year, and it is only the fertilised queens which survive the winter in hibernation. Small nests containing only a queen at the beginning of the season can be destroyed using a powerful aerosol wasp spray with caution.

Larger nests should be destroyed as a matter of urgency by a competent person who is equipped for the job.

Gardening terms[11]

Types of soil	
Acid Soil	Sol acide (m) – acidité
Clay	Argile (f)
Sand	Sable (m) (sable gras – loamy sand)
Chalky	Calcaire
Loam / potting compost	Terreau (m)
Topsoil	Couche (f) arable
Window box	Jardinière à plantes

---

[11] This list was compiled by the ACIP* Gardening Group.

Organic Fertilisers

Ash:	La cendre
Bone meal:	La poudre d'os, la farine d'os
Compost:	Le composte
Fertiliser:	Engrais
Green manure:	Engrais vert
Horn meal:	La corne torréfiée
Liquid plant feed:	Le purin de plante
Mulch:	Le paillage
Manure:	Le fumier
Poultry manure:	Le fumier de volaille
Seaweed:	Une algue
Horn and Blood	La corne et sang

Vegetables

Artichoke:	Un artichaut
Asparagus:	L'asperge
Bean:	Le haricot
Beetroot:	La betterave
Broadbean	La fève
Cabbage: / Cauliflower	Le chou / le chou-fleur
Celeriac	Le céleri-rave
Chard:	La bette or blette
Chilli	Le piment
Garlic / young garlic	L'ail / l'aillet
Jerusalem artichoke:	Le topinambour
Lamb's lettuce	La mâche
Leek:	Le poireau
Lettuce	La laitue
Marrow:	La courge
New Zealand spinach	Le tétragone
Onion:	Un oignon
Parsnip:	Le panais
Pea:	Le pois
Pepper (sweet):	Le poivron

Vegetables

Potato	La pomme de terre
Pumpkin:	Le potiron, la citrouille
Spinach	L'épinard (m)
Sprouts:	Les choux de Bruxelles
Swede:	Le rutabaga
Sweet corn	Le maïs doux
Sweet potato	La patate douce
Turnip:	Le navet
Horseradish	Le raifort

Fruit and fruit trees

Almond	L'amande / L'amandier
Apple	La pomme / le pommier
Apricot	L'abricot / l'abricotier
Blackberry / blackberry bush	Le mûr, la ronce
Blackcurrant	Le cassis, le cassissier
Cherry	La cerise / le cerisier
Morello Cherry	La griotte / le griottier
Cherry plum green/yellow/pink	La mirabelle
Sweet Chestnut	La châtaigne / le marronnier
Damson	La prune de damas /Quetsche
Fig	La figue / le figuier
Gooseberry	La groseille a maquereau
Hazel nut/tree	La noisette / le noisetier
Lemon	Le citron, le citronnier
Lime	Le citron vert, / le limier, (*not tilleul, which is the other kind of lime/linden tree*)
Medlar	La nèfle / le néflier
Mulberry	La mûre / le mûrier

Fruit and fruit trees

Nectarine	La nectarine/ le nectarinier
Nectarine /brugnon[12]	La brugnon / le brugnonier
Orange – Seville(bitter) Orange	L'orange – l'orange amère
Peach	La pêche /le pêcher
Plum	La prune / le prunier
Pomegranate	La grenade / le grenadier
Pear	La poire / le poirier
Quince	Le coing / le cognassier
Raspberry	La framboise / le framboisier
Redcurrant	La groseille à grappes / Le groseillier
Walnut	La noix / le noyer
Nuttery (Walnuts)	La noyeraie
Sloe (blackthorn)	La prunelle / le prunellier

[12] The brugnonier (which gives nectarines/brugnons, with flesh that adheres to the stones) and the nectarine (which gives nectarines, with free stones) both belong to the species *Prunus persica, variety nucipersica*. These fruits with smooth skin and yellow or white flesh are variants of the peach

Fences, hedging & coppicing

Coppicing	Le recépage
hedges	La haie
Copse shoots from the bottom)	La cépée
Fence	La clôture
Raised earth bank	Le talus
Ditch	Le fossé
Pollarded tree (shoots from the top)	Le têtard, ragosse, bulteau
Low wall	Le muret

Garden Tools

Spade	La bêche
Fork	La fourche
Rake	Le râteau
Hoe	La houe, la binette
Secateurs	Le sécateur
Shredder	Le broyeur
Strimmer	La débroussailleuse
Lawn Mower	La tondeuse

Watering and Irrigation

Hosepipe	Le tuyau d'arrosage
Sprinkler	L'arrosage par aspersion/diffusion
Water (to)	Arroser
Watering can	Un arrosoir
Watering rose	Une pomme d'arrosoir
Drip system	Le goutte à goutte
A meal 'well-watered' with alcohol	Un repas bien arrosé

Miscellaneous

Lawn	La pelouse
Bug	La punaise
Maggot	L'asticot
Cutting	La bouture
Windbreak	Un brise-vent
Root	La racine
Lime	Chaux (f) agricole
Annual	Plante annuelle (f)
Bud	Bourgeon (m)
Cordon	Cordon (m)
Dormant	Endormi / au repos
Evergreen	À feuilles persistantes
Deciduous	À feuilles caduques
Fumigate	Fumiger
Grafting	Greffe (f)
Hardy	Résistant(e) au gel, vivace, rustique
Lateral	Latéral(e)
Bare-rooted tree	Un arbre à racines nues

Gardening activities/verbs

To garden	Jardiner
To plant	Planter
To dig	Bêcher
To sow	Semer
To hoe	Houer, biner
To water	Arroser
To weed	Désherber, arracher les mauvais herbes
To rake	Râteler, ratisser
To shovel up	Ramasser, entasser à la pelle
To fork in, to fork over	Remuer
To fertilise	Fertiliser
To pinch off a bud	Épincer un bourgeon
To prick out	Repiquer des plants
To dead head/trim/prune	Tailler, élaguer
To mow	Tondre
To prune a branch	Élaguer une branche
To pollenate	Polliniser
To pick (flowers or fruit)	Cueillir
To harvest / collect	Ramasser - récolter
To ridge or earth up	Buttage

DIY

Do-it-yourself has not been as popular in France as in the UK or the USA, but it is rapidly catching on with make-over programmes frequently shown on TV.

France is the land of artisans who are proud of what they do. They take their time, have a reputation for arriving when they please and are quite expensive but do a good job, with incoming nationalities gaining the reputation of 'cow-boys'. However, in the last 10 years DIY stores have arrived with a vengeance and are now enormous. They no longer close for the whole of August, they open at lunchtimes, you can order on-line and collect at their 'Drive' within a couple of hours of ordering. Here are a few quirks to be aware of.

Gaine[13]

The French electrical system is quite different from the 'ring main' system used in the UK, and is more like a star, with one wire coming from the fuse box to each socket. Apart from this being an entire subject for experts, with 'norms' seeming to change every month, the one thing noticeable to the casual observer is the use of the grey '*gaine*' used to lay the cable throughout the house. So, you can end up with a massive bundle of cables and '*gaines*' coming into your fuse box.

This '*gaine*' is used in different colours for different purposes, so, if you find red gaine in the garden that means there are electrical cables inside. If blue then the '*gaine*' is protecting water supply and if green it is protecting communication cables, such as telephone or ethernet

---

[13] Important: Unless your electricity is installed by a certified electrician, I am told your house insurance is INVALID

cables, and yellow designates gas-pipes. In the house, copper pipes which are laid under the floor, for example, are protected by *'gaine'* as well – red *'gaine'* for hot water and blue *'gaine'* for cold. Of course, you can't rely on this as it's not unknown for builders to run out of the right colour and use whatever they can lay their hands on, and perhaps use a bit of tape on the end to signify the difference. Neither is it unheard of to save money by only using *'gaine'* on the last metre or so that it passes inspection.

'Grillage Avertisseur'

Another thing you might come across when digging up your garden is plastic tape/grill which is laid a few centimetres above underground cables to warn you of what lies below. Again, this is colour coded.

French windows – *'porte-fenêtre'*

French windows can be very heavy depending on the size and the number of panels and they come locked. My better half thought we could manage moving the French windows off the trailer *'remorque'*, by taking the panels out, moving the frame and then putting the door panels back. But getting the doors out of the frame seemed impossible. They do not come with door furniture such as handles and lock barrels. These must be ordered separately.

Unless you have the foresight to order lock barrels and door handles at the same time as the windows, you have no way of removing the door panels. Of course, if you already have French doors installed on your property it is possible to remove a door handle and an existing lock barrel, insert them into the new French doors and unlock the lock, open the doors and remove them. It's a bit of a puzzle the first time you come across this.

Firewood – 'bois de chauffage'

Wood stoves, log burners and 'inserts' (a log burner built into the chimney) are still a prime way to heat your home in rural France. But perhaps for not much longer as some countries (but not France) are now trying to ban them because it is said that, for example, 40% of particle emissions in the UK are caused by solid fuel burning. However, the French have defined wood as a renewable source. They diligently plant young trees to replace those felled. It's not unusual for ex-pats to be horrified at the great expanses of felled tree, and huge piles of logs on the side of the road, as they do not understand that trees like these are just another crop.

Best types of wood to burn

It is important to burn dry wood (less than 20% humidity). Wood which is not dry burns but produces tar and blackens the stove window. In addition, it creates a lot of ash and does not heat up. Newcomers in France often want to burn pine, because it's cheap. Luckily most wood suppliers will refuse to supply it. They know that comparatively little heat is given off by pine or by fruit wood although it smells nice. Pine also can cause chimney fires, by clogging them up with unburnt tar and resin. The most calorific species is beech 'hêtre' followed by oak 'chêne', hornbeam 'charme' and ash 'frêne'. Acacia is also good as is chestnut 'châtaigne', but you can only use chestnut in a closed wood burner 'poêle', rather than an open fire because it tends to spark badly.

Importance of regular chimney sweeping

It's very important to have your chimney swept each year (or to use a *'bûche de ramonage'* with a certificate – this is a special 'chimney sweeping log' that helps to keep your chimney clean between physical sweepings) as the validity of your house insurance depends on it. This applies to open fires as well as log burning stoves and inserts.

How wood is measured

The term *'stère'* is still used to sell wood, even though it was banned in December 1977. A *'stère'* is the equivalent of a cubic metre of logs cut to 1 metre lengths. A *'brasse'* is four *'stères'* of wood.

Stères

There is a problem with measuring wood by the stère/m3 because it depends on the length of logs used, If the size of the logs is less than 1 metre, the apparent volume of wood decreases because the voids are better filled. Thus the 'stère' no longer corresponds to 1 cubic metre, but to 0.8 of a cubic metre for logs in 50-centimetre lengths, and 0.7 of a cubic metre for logs in 33cm lengths and 0.6 of a cubic metre for logs cut to 25cm. Yet you have the same amount of wood

In France everything is made a bit harder if you don't speak the language quite fluently. Translation/ *'traduction'* tools help to give you the gist, but equally they can cause some problems. Just recently my husband decided to chivvy up the woodman for the second half of our delivery of firewood. The remaining 4 *'brasses'* which should have been here in May, and still hadn't arrived in December. He composed his message in English, spelling *'brasse'* incorrectly as 'bras' and then he used Google Translate to put the message into French and send this SMS, pictured, and got a suitable reply: Please note, this will only be amusing to those with a reasonable grasp of French and English.

Good day,
When can you deliver the other 4 bras? *(soutiens-gorge?)*
If all goes well before new year. Frank

Ok no worries but I do not have bras to sell

Auto-translate is marvellous isn't it?

After consultation with a few feminists, they assure me that burning their bras is liberating, but they don't have the same calorific value as wood.
Therefore I'd like 4 brasse of wood in their place.
Thanks. Frank

Waste collection and recycling

In rural France you are unlikely to have your waste collected but you will find '*poubelles*' - locations with coloured coded bins called '*bennes*'. Until recently ordinary household waste has been collected in black plastic bags and deposited in the black-lidded bins. A new system is being introduced during 2020 where householder are issued with a keycard/badge which enables you to dispose of up to 60 litres 24 times a year for a couple or 48 times a year for a family of 4 in the '*benne noire*'. With a charge at the end of the year of between €145 - €250 per year. Extra openings will cost between €3 and €4.

Recyclable rubbish was collected in yellow plastic bags '*sacs jaunes*' which, in our area, you obtained from the local *Mairie* or post office. These were then deposited in the bins with yellow lids. Now you will be expected to bring your recyclables and deposit them in one of three '*bennes*' – 'paper and recyclable plastics', cartons, and glass.

If you have big items to get rid of, then the '*déchetterie*' (waste recycling centre) is the place for you. You can get rid of most things there, including asbestos, but not cars. They are well organised, with labelled skips for everything, so you must sort your rubbish before you go. They do have skips with '*tout venant*' (everything) for all the odds and ends but you can be sent home to get organised before they will accept your rubbish. Some '*déchetteries*' will let you in and just make a note of your commune, others will require a card that shows you are local and have the right to use their facility. They also have limits as to how many times or how much rubbish you can dump in a week.

Confusing English

The French love it if you take a dish of something typically 'English (by which they mean Scottish, Irish, Welsh or English)' to an event. By that they don't mean 'curry' or other 'foreign' food we typically eat in UK – oh no that won't do at all.

Things like Cheddar are accepted but not nearly so happily as Stilton. Shortbread is always a hit. The term 'pudding' is used as a term of derision. I think we British use it as an alternative to 'dessert', and don't necessarily mean steamed pudding. But all the French I know think we only eat steamed pudding and Christmas pudding. Heavy.

They laugh at the way we call 'dessert' desert – they think we are talking about the Sahara (pronounced *'saara'*) – a waitress will be amused to tell her compatriots that 'that table over there wants a plate of sand'. They make the double 'ss' into a 'sssss' as in serpent.

I took some mince pies into my pottery class just before Christmas and they loved them. I had to explain that these days they don't have any minced meat in them – as once they did and the dried fruit was used to help cover the fact that the meat was perhaps not quite fresh.

My pottery teacher loves dunking her biscuits into tea, whilst her husband and I look on in horror, both she and my husband love the disgusting habit. I think she normally uses 'Speculos', a biscuit of Dutch origin, but my husband assured her that the best biscuit to dunk was a gingernut, and not long after bought a packet at the supermarket to give her. "And what kind of nuts do they have in gingernuts?" she asked. "Err – there are no nuts in gingernuts" was the reply. "English is a very strange language, where mince pies have no mince and ginger nuts have no nuts", she said. Also, ginger is considered an aphrodisiac therefore ginger nuts can cause laughing fits!

Pouces

I was in an Art class recently and our course leader mentioned her surprise that TV screens over here are still measured in inches '*pouces*'. It's not just TV screens but computer screens too. The French word '*pouce*' also means thumb.

As well as computer and TV screens, car tyres are partly measured in inches. The first 2 numbers are in millimetres and refer to the width and profile of the tyre the next number is the diameter of the wheel in inches!

Paperwork and admin.

This book does not intend to be a formal and complete guide to the law in France, as everything changes constantly and on 1st of each month there is always a raft of new laws, covering everything from healthcare, to minimum wage (SMIC) to vehicle testing, speed limits, price competition and so on. Each month "The Local", publishes a list of changes coming up that month – see https://www.thelocal.fr. A good source of information in English is the UK government web site: https://www.gov.uk/guidance/living-in-france. Other good sources of up-to-date information are the various guides published by the Connexion English Language newspaper - https://www.connexionfrance.com/. Of course, there are many books published on 'Buying Property in France', 'Living in France', 'Renovating in France' and so on which can be found on Amazon, some of which are updated regularly.

The sections below, therefore, provide a personal experience which may differ widely in the various prefectures in France, and with the changing status of the UK in relation to Europe, but can provide some valuable pointers. If you do what is asked it is usually straightforward. However, one thing to note for married women, is the need to always have proof of how your maiden name has changed to your married name – or whatever name you use today (for example, if you have changed the way your name is spelt). This will not necessarily be listed on the list of required documents. For example, before this was done online, when my husband and I queued up to change our driving licences, my husband in front of me sailed through and got his French licence. I was next and got rejected as I did not have my marriage certificate with me. Even with passport and husband there, I still had to prove how my name had gone from my maiden name – which French women retain on marriage and appears on all their documents - to my married name.

Besides this non-national married women need their Marriage Certificate, to prove how their name has changed from the name on their birth certificate to their married name – if that is what appears on their driving licence and/or passport. Of course, if there are any other name changes, be it by divorce or deed-poll, you need the documents to prove the name trail.

More and more administration is being carried out online, where, until recently, it was handled at the Prefectures. You will hear people talking about the ANTS system, or the '*Agence Nationale des Titres Sécurisés*'. This system is used to apply for driving licences (if you've just passed your test, need a periodic medical, need to add points or delete them), carte grise (if lost or stolen, or you have bought or sold a car, changed your address etc), visas and boat licences. It is also used for French citizens to apply for birth certificates, passports and national identity cards. From March 2020 it will also be used to change your driving licence from an English to a French one.

The ANTS[14] system can be logged into using your Ameli.fr account details, or your login for the tax website, or a few others using "*FranceConnect*", which saves having to keep yet another set of login details.

---

[14] https://ants.gouv.fr/

Residence Permit and money transactions

Applying for a Carte de Séjour or Residence Permit can be more difficult for women, particularly married women because in France the man still reigns supreme, which means it is the husband's name that automatically appears on insurance documents and utility contracts unless the contrary is clearly specified at the outset.

So, when you come to France make sure your name is included jointly on all the utility bills, and make sure your name is spelled correctly. You will need those bills to prove you are living here on a regular basis.

If you are trying to make any financial transactions, for example transferring money from one country to another, or trying to buy and sell shares on-line, for money-laundering purposes you will have to provide documentation, such as utility bills in your own name.

Until now, applying for a Titre de Séjour has not been difficult for a UK citizen. For a start, it is free, secondly, nothing has to be translated into French, unlike visas for Third Country Nationals (TCNs).

Following the Brexit Withdrawal Agreement (WA) a new acronym arrived with the new system for Britons applying for a carte de séjour - WARP – Withdrawal Agreement Residence Permit.

Currently, and until June 2021 British citizen can continue to live in France and can also travel to and from France freely without the need for a carte de séjour, otherwise known as a Residence Permit.

The French have excelled themselves in making new on-line system remarkably simple and straightforward.

A voluntary organisation known as RIFT (Remain in France Together) have produced some excellent documents regarding the process of obtaining the new "WARPs" here:

https://www.remaininfrance.fr/wapermitprocessoverview

This document walks you through the process of obtaining a card, in English, and what documents you need to produce depending on your individual circumstances. I will not attempt to repeat what is discussed so lucidly in the above document here, save to mention two points of confusion I have heard discussed a few times.

The first is a question near the beginning of the process which asks if this is the first time you have applied. It means to this specific process, not if you have applied for a residence card before via any other system.

Secondly, something that does not translate well – when the French ask for your name "nom", they mean your surname, and in the case of married women your maiden name. Next, the username, the name you are generally known as, for married women, that is your husband's surname if you use it. After that they want to know your first names. If you put your name in as say "Joe Bloggs", and then your first name in as Joe, your attestation at the end of the process will be shown as Joe Bloggs Joe.

For Third Country Nationals (TCNs) the process is more complex, has costs associated with it, and documents must be formally translated into French. Visas must be applied for at the French embassy in the country you are living in before coming to France. For many a short visit for up to 90 days does not need a visa. For more details there is the French government's guide, in English, which indicates who needs a visa, how to go about it and associated documents required:

https://france-visas.gouv.fr/en_US/web/france-visas/visa-application-guidelines.

The health system

One of the magnificent things about France, is their health system. Although like the NHS, it is beginning to creak under the strain, you still get seen far more quickly than in the UK. The paragraphs below give you a general outline of the situation in France as we have experienced it, but you would do well to get detailed info from specialised sites, as every month there are new rules and regulations and the situation with Brexit as I write could have a big impact.

The system of health care in France is known as *'l'assurance maladie'*, and since 1st January 2016 France has had in place a universal system of healthcare, called the *Protection Universelle Maladie* (PUMa). The law merely requires that in order to validate your rights you must have been resident for a minimum of three months and then live in France for at least six months a year. Those who hold an S1 certificate of entitlement (e.g. retirees from UK) will only nominally be affiliated to PUMa (for administrative purposes), as European Regulations grant them and their family members an entitlement to health cover via the certificate. S1 households do not pay a charge to the French health system and they are also exempt from social charges on their pension, otherwise there is a PUMa *'cotisation'* to pay, which is currently being much debated, but is not payable if you have a low income.

If you need help regarding your *'Carte Vitale'* there is an English-speaking helpline 09 74 75 36 46 (00 33 9 74 75 36 46 from outside France) who provide a really good service and advice. There are also some web pages in English https://www.ameli.fr/assure/english-pages. These pages cover more than nine areas of interest.

You can register for French healthcare via your local CPAM (*Caisse Primaire Assurance Maladie*) office.

If you are a British retiree, then you will need to provide:

- Your SI from the Dept of Work and Pensions (until Brexit 00441903529066 option 5)

- CERFA form (Cerfa 60-3406 Déclaration en vue de l'immatriculation d'un pensionné.)

- Passport

- Birth certificate

- Proof of residence in France for more than 3 months (e.g. Attestation from EDF)

- Bank RIB

- Declaration de '*médecin traitant*' (the name the doctor you have signed up with)

It takes about 4-5 weeks to be included in the healthcare system and then another 3-4 weeks to get your '*carte vitale*'. Once you have registered, you will be issued with a Carte Vitale[15] which is the size of a credit card, which you use everywhere – at the doctors, the pharmacy, the hospital, the dentist, the specialist. You will need it for treatment in hospital, and sometimes lab tests. If you have extra insurance, you will need to show proof of this as well.

If you are employed, your employer will probably sort this out for you, but it is your responsibility to make sure this happens.

If you are self-employed there are different organisations who take care of this, depending on your 'metier' and the type of business you are setting up.

---

[15] April 2019 new plans to digitise the health system were announced which reveals there will no need to have a physical card and instead everything will be online, with a carte vitale app "apCV" set to be tested summer 2019 for roll out by 2021.

Unlike the UK where healthcare is free at point of use, in France you normally pay, except for conditions when you are covered '100%' (*cent pour cent*) (with certain medical conditions, such as cancer and chronic conditions you don't have to pay up front, so called ALD – '*Affection de Longue Durée*'). Since the end of 2017, a new system has been rolled out where doctors and certain medical personnel no longer charge upfront but are paid directly by the government or health insurer – essentially meaning 'free' doctor visits.

Your carte vitale ensures that you will get large percentage of medical costs back in your bank account very quickly or even find you don't have to pay at all. Any remaining amount can be covered by taking out a '*mutuelle*' or a top-up insurance. There is a difference between the 2 types of organisation which provide this type of cover but, either way they will refund most or all the remaining cost. You aren't required to have a *mutuelle*, otherwise known as complimentary health cover and there are many different schemes, but the one outstanding difference between private health insurance in UK and a France is that they are not allowed here to exclude pre-existing conditions! Note that refunds are based on a tariff published by the government. If you see a consultant who charges over the recognised tariff then, unless you have a very good top up insurance, the portion above the tariff will not be refunded. This is known as '*Dépassement d'Honoraires*':

Dépassement d'honoraires

'*Dépassement d'honoraires*' or excess fees are sometimes charged by doctors, consultants and surgeons. A fee overrun is the difference between the conventional fee for a health benefit (defined by Social Security) and the actual amount billed to the patient. Example: the conventional price of a consultation of a general practitioner in metropolitan France is 25€. Any excess fees are not covered by Social

Security *'l'assurance maladie'* but may be reimbursed by some complementary health policies.

Until you get cover here you can get emergency cover using your EHIC (European Health Insurance Card), which is issued in the UK and lasts for 5 years. (This may of course change after Brexit.) The EHIC is replaced by the French CEAM (*Carte Européenne d'Assurance Maladie*) equivalent for people who are living and working in France (i.e. for people not on an S1). It covers you for emergency health care when you travel out of France into the EU and associated countries. Currently, when you retire and get your S1 you revert to the EHIC issued in the UK. Again, you won't be reminded so you must remember to apply yourself. You can apply for your CEAM online through your Ameli.fr account. (short for *Assurance Maladie*). To set up such an account go to the ameli.fr website and they will ask for the following information – I'm showing it in 'English', but it will be in French:

If you have extra insurance, then each year it must be validated at your local *pharmacie* (chemist), so that your Carte Vitale and your insurer can be linked together on your ameli.fr record. After that you

don't need to take the *mutuelle* with you to the *pharmacie*.

General practitioner - *médecin traitant*

These days you are expected to sign up with a *'généraliste'* / *médecin traitant* (GP). This is recorded on your computer record at Ameli.fr. The *médecin traitant* will then decide which specialists you need to see and issue an introductory letter accordingly. You can make an appointment directly with a specialist but sometimes the full cost is not then reimbursed. You can contact the dentist and *opthalmologiste* directly and be reimbursed.

Eye tests – *ophtalmologiste*

Note, there is one big difference between France and the UK. To get your eyes tested you make an appointment with an ophtalmologiste. They test your eyes using a vast array of equipment and then issue a prescription *'ordonnance'* which you take to your local opticians which has the glasses *'lunettes'*, contact lenses *'lentilles de contact'* soft *'souples'*. They can work from a UK prescription, but although there is some difference between the way things are written on the prescriptions, most seem to cope. By UK standards most opticians are very expensive, and often the reimbursement is laughably small, so many people buy on-line or wait until they go back to the UK. However, there are a few more inexpensive opticians starting up and Macron has vowed to get the price of glasses and hearing aids reduced.

District Nurses - *infirmière*

Another difference between France and the UK is that 'district nurses' *'infirmièr(e)'* who work outside hospitals are mainly self-employed or attached to doctors' surgeries. So, if you come home from an operation and you have been given a prescription to have someone come and change your dressings for the next 10 days, for example, don't just sit there and wait for someone to turn up, as you would in the NHS. You must find a local *infirmièr(e)* and call them to make an appointment to come to see you. They will need the *ordonnance* (prescription) and your *carte vitale*. If you have come home from an operation in hospital it may be that you need dressings changed, antiseptic and various supplies. If so, you will be issued with an ordonnance for these as well which need to be collected from the pharmacy ready for the nurse to use. These nurses work extremely hard and are prepared to come to your home to take blood samples, give infirm people showers, even collect prescriptions, but there is a small charge for this service.

Blood tests

As well as having a nurse come and take a blood test, you can also go to your local laboratory *'laboratoire'* if you know one, which is free if you have a *carte vitale*. Results are either posted to you, can be collected, or these days can be emailed to you (and your GP) that afternoon.

In France you are responsible for looking after your own health records. If you are sent for a scan or an x-ray for example, you will be expected to wait for the results, perhaps for 20 minutes or half an hour, and you take them home with you and then take them to your GP *'généraliste'* or specialist.

Donating Blood – *'don du sang'*

If you have spent one year or more in the UK between 1980-1996, you cannot give blood or plasma in France. This is because they are afraid of catching mad-cow disease from us.

Dossier médical partagé

Currently there is an on-going project to collect medical records for the whole population – DMP or *Dossier médical partagé*. The Shared Medical Record (DMP) is a digital health record that keeps your health information: treatments, test results, allergies. It allows you to share your records with the health professionals of your choice, who may need them to treat you.

Changes to the system precipitated by COVID-19

During the lockdown (le confinement) in France, everyone has become increasingly interested in using on-line methods of communicating. One of these is to use Doctolib.fr website (or download their mobile application), where you can search for a doctor in your area, either to make appointments or whether video consultations are available (sometimes they will want to see you in person if you are over the age of 70 for example). Admittedly the take up of this service, by the medical profession, is greater in large conurbations than in rural areas. Check whether they will take your Carte Vitale "Carte Vitale acceptée", whether they are sector 1 or 2 etc.

If they give you a prescription "an ordonnance" it is not necessary to print it, you can simply show it on your mobile screen or send it via email when you arrive at a clinic. There is a function on Doctolib to share your prescription.

An alternative is to use Qare.fr. This provides a tele-consultation service with a choice of doctors in specialist areas. Again, check if they take your Carte Vitale, whether they will issue sicknotes. Your ordonnance is delivered to your device via the app together with the fiche to reclaim. Excellent for out of hours.

Consumer Organisations

60 millions de consommateurs – (60 millions consumers) or *Que Choisir* (What to choose)

The magazine '*60 millions de consommateurs*' and its associated web-site are published by the National Institute of Consumers '*l'Institut national de la consommation*', one of whose main missions is to 'gather, produce, analyse and disseminate information, studies, surveys and tests.

The range of articles and surveys covered is huge.

'*Que Choisir*' is another subscription-based body that tests and compares and gives their independent opinion on the products and services of your everyday life. They even provide standard letters for things like termination or disputes.

'*Familles de France*'. Consumer Organisation

If you ever need some help or advice, without going to your *notaire*, one option might be to contact '*Familles de France*'. Originally set up to help large families, this organisation can help in all sorts of ways for a relatively small fee of €25; whether consumer, housing or family problems, banking or internet or utilities.

SOLVIT

Unfair rules or decisions and discriminatory red tape can make it hard for you to live, work or do business in another EU country. So, if you as an EU citizen or business face extra obstacles in another country because a public authority isn't doing what is required under EU law, SOLVIT can help by reminding authorities in question what your EU rights are and works with them to solve your problem. See:

http://ec.europa.eu/solvit/index_en.htm

Typical issues SOLVIT can help you with:

Getting your professional qualifications recognised

Visa & residence rights

Trade & services (businesses)

Family benefits

Pension rights

Working abroad

Unemployment benefits

Health insurance

Access to education

Cross-border movement of capital or payments

VAT refunds.

Travel Cards – oui.sncf

If you travel by train or bus you might find it worth getting a travel card. Senior citizen (from 60 years) cards benefit from a 25% reduction guaranteed in 2nd class and up to -40% in 1st, as well as benefits on services. There are discount cards available for other ages as well.

https://en.oui.sncf/en/discount-cards/sale/#/carte-senior/purchase

The Postal System

'*La poste*' – the postal system here is very good, especially in rural areas, where many delivery drivers may have great difficulty finding you if you do not have a street address. Many people live in so called '*lieu dits*' (known as...) (L.D.) which is smaller than a commune. Often there are no road/street names or numbers and no house names, and only the local *facteur* (postman) knows where people live.

One alternative to having things posted to your home address is to use a 'relay point'. There are many of these, in places like *tabacs* and paper shops and it saves having to wait in for a delivery. The other reason for using the relay points is that returns are free, whereas the cost of postage is very high.

Often it is much cheaper to go online and use an organisation such as 'Parcel Monkey', or 'Mondial Relay'. Depending on the organisation you choose, parcels can be deposited at a local relay point or the items may still go via '*Chronopost*' (the parcel delivery arm of La Poste), and still be deposited at the local post office, but you can arrange it all online and pay for it online. The 'relay' system works when dealing with French catalogue companies and Amazon.fr. Unfortunately, companies outside France, like Amazon.co.uk, don't currently use these relay points, and they either use delivery companies or La Poste, the latter tending to be more reliable in rural areas.

If you want to terminate a contract, then you will need to send the letter via recorded delivery '*lettre Recommandée avec accusé de Reception*' (RAR).

CESU - (Chèque emploi service universel)

This is the official system to use when employing casual labour (work around the house, baby-sitting, dog-walking, private lessons, home help and small gardening jobs).

Rather than employing people on the 'black' this system has the advantage that the employee is covered in case of accident or injury within the French social security system, and the employer benefits from a substantial tax reduction and is insured in case of damage caused by the employee.

You pay in cash or by cheque and declare the payments on the CESU website. CESU will charge you the social security contribution through direct debit. Depending on the service, you get income tax relief on the payments automatically.

You can access CESU website via smartphone or tablet as well as PC. For more information see www.cesu.urssaf.fr

Note: The CESU is part of URSSAF (*Union de recouvrement des cotisations de sécurité sociale et d'allocations familiales*) which is the main social security office for all businesses in France and their role includes collection of funds, control of contributions and dealing with litigation.

Buying and using English computers in France.

There are some issues with using existing computers in France as well as considerations when buying new or getting them fixed. If this subject makes your eyes glaze over then just observe the following:

1. If you want to type on an English keyboard with English menus in your programs, buy on Amazon or somewhere similar, making sure you get a warranty that works in France.

2. Use "Insert symbols" in Word to get your accents

3. Make sure you have an anti-virus program running, there are good ones available which are free, e.g. Sophos or Avast

4. Make sure you keep backups of anything important, you can do this to the "cloud", e.g. OneDrive, Google Drive or Drop Box,

5. Get yourself a password manager to store those passwords you are sure to forget e.g. Password Plus

The rest of this chapter expands on the points above and can be skipped if your eyes glaze over.

If you are British you will probably be used to a UK QWERTY keyboard, that does have a £ sign and a € sign, but no accent keys for the likes of é. If you are American you will probably have a US QWERTY keyboard, with no £ and no accent keys.

If you buy a computer in France it will come with an AZERTY keyboard, that does have most of the French accented keys, and they "might" sell you a QWERTY keyboard as an optional add-on - not exactly what you want if you are a laptop user, and not at all helpful if you are a touch-typist. If you are buying an Apple then you can specify the keyboard that you want, on their website.

Also, if you are buying a French version of Windows, and you want an English version, you will have to buy a separate licence.

My advice to people is to buy on Amazon UK (or somewhere similar) and personal experience dictates you buy from Amazon themselves, not a marketplace seller who can be much less inclined to provide support if the hardware has a fault. Make sure that any warranty will work in France.

Typing Accented characters

If you are typing on an Android device like a smartphone or tablet, then you have it easy, as you can just hold down the key, for example 'a' and you will get 10 choices of 'a' each with a different accent. If you

are typing on an Android device like a smartphone or tablet, then you have it easy, as you can just hold down the key, for example 'a' and you will get 10 choices of 'a' each with a different accent.

Likewise, with an iPad the simplest way is just to hold-down the character key and a pop-up menu will offer all the available accents (not just French) with a number. Press the number and you get the accented character.

Typing accented characters on a QWERTY keyboard

If you are typing on a QWERTY keyboard on a PC then life is a bit more tedious, but you do have 5 ways of making accented keys. Unless you are especially interested, I suggested the first option "Insert symbol" is the easiest to remember and skip the rest which I leave below for the sake of the "few".

Insert Symbol

If you are in an application like Word, you can simply select "Insert" and then "Symbols" and again "Symbol" and select the character you want. This works for things like "degrees" (°), half (½) etc., and copyright symbols, not just accented characters. But it takes several clicks to get what you want.

Enable the onboard US International keyboard

Enabling the onboard *Windows US International keyboard* allows you to type a combination of 2 characters to create the accented letters. This is probably the best method if you are going to be typing accents often. It is also the best method if you have a laptop without a numeric keypad.

First there is the one-time task of enabling the keyboard. After that you just must get used to using the key combinations.

To enable the US International keyboard, do this:

- Click on the start button (bottom left of screen)

- Click on Settings (the gear wheel immediately above the on/off button)

- Click on *"Time & Language"*, then

- Click on *"Region and Language"* and you will be shown the language you have set up on your PC for your location and for your content.

- Beneath the "Add a language button" there is a list of keyboards you use. Do **not** "Add a language" – instead click on whatever keyboard you have set up. Mine is "English United Kingdom – Windows Display language" and an *"Options"* button will appear.

- Under options choose *"United States International QWERTY"*.

- On the right of your taskbar, at the bottom of the screen, the option will appear where you can then toggle between keyboards – ENG INTL or ENG UK.

With the "United States International QWERTY" keyboard, option ENG INTL, enabled you just use:

- the apostrophe for acute *"aigu"* accent [é, ú, í, ó, á] plus cedilla [ç] *"cédille"* and

- the grave accent at the top left [next to the 1 on the numbers row] for grave accents [è, ù, ì, ò, à].

- For umlauts *"tréma"* use the double quote on the "2" key for [ë, ÿ, ü, ï, ö, ä],

- Use the carat key for accent *"circonflexe"* (above the 6) for [ê, û, î, ô, â]

Having selected ENG INTL, when you press these accent keys nothing is displayed on the screen until you press a second key:

- If you press one of the letters designated as eligible to receive an accent mark, the accented version of the letter appears.

- If you press the key of a character that is not eligible to receive an accent mark, two separate characters appear.

- If you press the space bar, the symbol (apostrophe, quotation mark, accent grave, tilde, accent circumflex or caret) is displayed by itself.

Note, you will find that the @ sign (on the apostrophe key) and the double quote " on the 2 key will have swapped places, and the hash becomes a forward slash – otherwise they are pretty similar.

Using your **numeric** keypad

Another way is to use your **numeric** keypad and use a 4-digit code for the character you want. These can be found bottom right of the character map circled in the screenshot above. For example, to type a small letter 'e' with a grave accent, hold down the 'alt' key and on the numeric keypad type '0232'. Personally, I find this method the easiest as I don't have to remember to select the ENG INTL keyboard. I have a 'post-it' with the 12 most common accented keys in French on my monitor.

I've just been informed by a reader in American of an alternative set of 3-digit codes that can be used with the Alt key on a numeric keypad. They have the advantage of only needing 3 digits rather than the four. They are listed along with the 4-digit codes below:

| Alt+ 0232
Alt+138 | è | Alt+ 0233
Alt+130 | é | Alt+0234
Alt+136 | ê |
| Alt+ 0224
Alt+ 133 | à | Alt+ 0226
Alt+ 131 | â | Alt+0231
Alt+ 135 | ç |

Alt+ 0246 Alt+ 148	ö	Alt+ 0244 Alt+ 147	ô	Alt +0251 Alt+ 150	û
Alt + 0239 Alt+ 139	ï	Alt+ 0238 Alt+ 140	î	Alt+ 0249 Alt+ 151	ù

The three-key combination

Another method is to use a three-key combination. For example, 'ctrl' + apostrophe and then 'a' will give you 'á', or 'ctrl' accent grave then and 'e' will give you è. These are shown in more detail below:

The important keys are:

- 'ctrl', and immediately above, the shift key,

- the grave accent key, top left under the 'esc' key,

- the caret (circumflex) '^' key, shares the number 6 key,

- the colon which is the diaeresis or 'tréma' key on its side effectively, and

- the apostrophe key which is used as an acute accent

So, to type 'è' (the example illustrated in the photo) you press '**ctrl+` +e**', or to type 'é' you press '**ctrl+'+e**'.

Other Computer considerations

Whilst in France you are just as likely to get viruses, breakdowns and forget your password as when you are in the UK.

Anti-virus software

Make sure your device is protected. Windows 10 has Windows Defender – at the very least make sure it is turned on. There are other options which are better. **Sophos**, a British product, has a free option for home users, and is highly recommended. **Avast** offers more security-enhancing features and, independent tests prove that Avast is better than Windows Defender in terms of both malware detection and the impact on system performance.

Backups

It is surprising how many people who fail to back-up their documents and photographs. A simple external hard drive used regularly, or a Dropbox account or other cloud storage could save a considerable amount of time, anguish and money (data recovery is time-consuming and will cost more than an external drive).

Passwords

When I'm asked for help, the first stumbling block is that nobody ever knows their passwords, and half a day is wasted trying to get a new password, because they've also forgotten the secondary questions that will be asked. Many folks think all this "password rubbish" is an imposition to be avoided at all costs. And, to fit in with this attitude up pops your browser offering to remember your passwords for you. Don't let it. It is only daily usage that you will assist your memory. I grant you it is tedious, but it is your data/money that is being protected.

Password Manager

Using your memory is easy advice if you only use one or two passwords, but every commercial site you visit will want a password, so the number you must remember will be probably in the hundreds and clearly, that is impractical. Especially since you shouldn't use the same password on more than one website.

The way around this is to use a "password manager" – there are lots out there – quite a few are free. The password manager enables you to keep a list of websites, banks, documents etc that need passwords or reference numbers. The password manager itself will have a password, and this is the only one you need to remember.

You will sometimes find password managers bundled with anti-virus software or may be provided as an app already installed on your smartphone.

Many of us have multiple devices, maybe a PC, a smartphone and a tablet. So, you need to keep your password manager on all of them and keep it synchronised, modern password apps are designed to do just that.

You may use a fingerprint to protect your phone or tablet. If not, you should try to use a pattern or PIN for your computer, phone and tablet, so they at least have a minimal amount of protection. It is important to remember what these are. Making your life easy by not having one, is to make life easy for anyone who pinches your phone.

It is also important to remember passwords for commonly used things like email, and of course your password manager. Email is especially important because that is where most commercial sites will send a link or code should you forget the password to their site. If you can't get into your email, then life gets so much harder.

Mobile phones and French SIMs

Many British hang on to their old UK phones and SIM cards, sometimes for more than 20 years. Perhaps this goes back to the days when PAYG cards in France only lasted for a month and any unused balance at the end of a month was forfeited rather than being brought forward (as in the UK) into the next month. However, times have changed and it is possible to get a contract (that can be ended whenever you like) for as little as €2 per month. Unless you have a contract with a phone that you are still paying off it really is worthwhile getting a French SIM and a French number as many couriers and delivery people cannot or will not call UK numbers, nor can, for example, Orange engineers. You don't have to buy a new phone as well, but you might have to get your current phone unlocked before purchasing a new SIM card.

Help when your French language skills are not great

When you don't speak good French life can get difficult, and you are constantly told to ask a neighbour for help, or consult professional translators, and sometimes this is the only thing to do. However, on a day-to-day basis, you can get a lot of help on your computer.

If you use the Google Chrome browser, there is an extension (Google Translate) you can install which will translate webpages for you into English (or some other language of your choosing). There is an option to automatically translate any web page written in French or you can choose when you want to translate a page, and you can toggle between the "original" language and the translation. Sometimes this is important to be able to understand what is really being said. Fluent French speakers usually jeer at the results, but if you are on your own, it can give you a sense of what is written. Of course, it can depend on how well written the original language text is too. I've found that more and more online French administrative pages – like your tax return – are written in a straightforward way that translates reasonably well.

If you have the Google Translate extension installed, and you read your email in the Chrome browser, you can use it to translate any French emails that you receive, by right-clicking anywhere in the email.

Another program (app) that is very useful is DeepL. There is a free and a paid version. Some folks rate the DeepL translations over Google Translate. You use DeepL by highlighting and copying the text you want translating and pasting it into the relevant box on the DeepL webpage, and it will translate in to English or vice versa – or Spanish into German etc.

Letter writing in France is fraught with difficulties, so if you want to write an important or official letter it is probably best to get help so that the right endings are included. There are sites that have examples of certain letters to the official bodies because they require a lot of official language and terms.

https://www.laposte.fr/courriers-colis/conseils-pratiques/rediger-une-lettre-formelle-quelles-formules-de-politesse

http://www.bienecrire.org/lettre-admin.php

So far, I have not found any help with using the telephone system, especially those which give you half a dozen choices before putting you through to someone. If you don't understand all the options given on the telephone my advice is to hang up and call again. Bit by bit you will understand all the choices. Another way is just to choose and if you get someone on the line, do excuse yourself and say you don't understand and usually they will connect you with the right person.

To help improve you French, other than getting lessons, subscribe to a magazine about something you are interested in, e.g., gardening, cooking, home improvements and try to read it. Listen to the radio. Watch French TV, particularly the news as you will probably have a good grasp of what they are talking about already.

Useful Books

- A large dictionary such as Le Robert & Collins, and Firefly French-English Visual Dictionary or French-English Bilingual Visual Dictionary (DK Bilingual Visual Dictionary), Leading dictionaries include Le Petit Larousse and Le Petit Robert Illustré, both around €30.

- The Connexion English Language Newspaper, besides being a monthly newspaper in English, has a big selection of books on specialist subjects such as top-up health care, how to fill in your tax return, inheritance and so on, and unlike a lot of books found on people's bookshelves, this information is kept up-to-date.

- Amazon has a huge range of books on Living in France. Most of them cover subjects like buying or renting a property, geography, money matters, insurance, wills, running a *gîte* and so on. Several of these are kept up to date.

Useful apps.

Microsoft Translator

This is a clever app that will let you speak a few words in English and immediately tell you what those words are in French (or Spanish or Greek), both written and spoken so you can get the pronunciation as well. It is also possible to type the words or photograph them, or indeed engage in a conversation with others via the app. And if you don't know what somebody is saying to you, you can ask them to speak to the smartphone and get the translation back. (It probably won't understand your poor accent.)

Météo France

If you're someone who likes to keep an eye on the weather around France, the Météo France app provides a ten-day forecast for France and around the world so you can follow the weather in your home country too. It's also handy for finding out when there are weather warnings in place for your area.

Oui.sncf

You can book trains, buses and air travel as well as accommodation and you'll get all the info you need, as well as the best prices.

RATP

The French capital's transport operator RATP's app, is handy for finding out how to get around Paris and the greater Paris region of Ile-de-France. You can also use it to find out the time of the next RER, Metro, bus and night buses, tram and airport lines.

SNCF

France's national rail company SNCF's app is useful if you tend to travel around the country by train. It gives you door-to-door itineraries and real-time information on your journeys even if you don't have a signal.

Ameli

Ameli is the website of the CPAM *'Caisse Primaire d'Assurance Maladie'* which is the organization dealing with state covered healthcare in France. You can find anything relating to your French healthcare admin. Ameli keeps track of all your personal health information, including your refunds.

C'est la grève

C'est la grève lists all the strikes going on across the country. You are alerted immediately to all strikes, when they are happening, where and the duration. It even allows you to select a geographic location to find out what's going on near you.

Impots.gouv

This app allows you to access your personal tax information quickly and easily. You can also use it for paying your taxes when the time comes.

Amendes.gouv

Traffic violations can be paid using this app rather than in person at a public revenue office, a tabac or by phone.

EDF & Moi

This gives access to your client 'space' at EDF, enabling you to look at your bills, enter your meter readings, download an *'Attestation'* or proof of home address, tell them if you are moving to a new house, details of your contract and so forth.

Ryanair

This is the easiest place to download, keep and show your boarding card.

Larousse French English Dictionary

Saves having to carry a paper dictionary around, and if you are connected to the internet, it can tell you how to pronounce words.

Linguee

Editorial dictionary – gives examples on the use of words.

Kindle

The kindle app is a great way to read a book on the go, taking no space in your bag. It is also a way of reading documents whilst away from the house or office if you email the document to the kindle app using the email address that is assigned by Amazon to all Kindle devices and Kindle apps.

Fitting in

Just as everyday life in Britain is very different depending on whether you live in a city or in a rural area, or indeed whether you come from "up north" or "down south", similarly you will find differences here in France. There are several customs which are universal, that you should be aware of:

Chrysanthemums

You see huge and impressive displays of these in the shops leading up to '*Toussaint*' – All Saints day - November 1st. These are intended strictly for the cemetery and not to be given in any circumstances as a gift, which would be an embarrassing social blunder or '*faux pas*' since they are closely associated with death.

Funerals

In small communes, when there is a funeral, the whole village is expected to attend, and your absence will be noted. If you are new to the area, someone may even come by and inform you or offer you a lift. So, if your French is not up-to-scratch, and that word '*obsèques*' keeps popping up in the conversation, nod sadly, rather than enthusiastically, and try to arrive at least at the beginning of the ceremony to sign the register of attendees. If you include your address, you normally receive a thank you card from the family whether you knew the person or not.

Armistice Day

This is another of those events that the whole community is expected to attend, and often there is a '*vin d'honneur*', a glass of wine, at the '*Mairie*' afterwards.

Chocolate

Milk chocolate tends to be for kids. If you are taking chocolates as a dinner gift, take dark chocolate.

Greetings

Everyone is expected to greet everyone they meet each day – even when walking into a shop. A simple *'bonjour – ca va'* at the very minimum with a kiss on each cheek[16] – more in some areas. It is only polite. It is a mistake to say *'bonjour'* again if you run into someone again later-on in the day – in that case it is *'re-bonjour'*. Waiting for the check-out staff to greet each other in the supermarket can make you impatient, but it is also one of the things that makes France charming.

---

[16] Kissing is for people you know, even slightly, otherwise a hand-shake – or even an elbow-shake for a workman with dirty hands.

Dealing with Death.

What happens, what needs to be done and how to proceed. This is not a complete guide; as always, everyone's experience is different, but here are the basics:

Be aware that you can reserve a plot in a cemetery for a very modest amount.

The first contact should be a doctor, who will sign the Death Certificate, *'declaration de décès'*.

If the person dies in hospital, the hospital will notify the *Mairie*. If the death occurred at home, the undertaker may do this for you. The *Mairie* can issue a multi-lingual copy of the Death Certificate, if appropriate, *'Formule Plurilingue de l'Acte de Décès'*. It's much cheaper to get a few copies of multi-lingual forms up-front.

It is advisable to obtain several original copies of all certificates (for example 20 copies) as these will be needed by the undertaker, French Social Security, health insurers, pension providers and those dealing with the estate back home.

Once the death has been registered at the *'Mairie'*, the burial permit *'permit d'inhumer'* will be issued.

There is a rule that the funeral needs to take place within 6 days. However, this can be easily extended with an extension from your prefecture which the undertaker *'Pompes Funèbres'* can request.

After death, the body will be transported to either a funeral parlour or home location.

At the undertaker's you will discuss all aspects of the funeral arrangements. You can choose the coffin, the coffin liner, what flowers you want, and if being cremated what urn you want. Don't be browbeaten into spending more than you want. You can go to a flower shop and make up your own bouquet at a more modest cost, for example.

The funeral could cost between €3000 and €5000. Rather than paying the bill yourself, it can be sent to the bank where the deceased had an account or to your *Notaire*. They will pay the bill directly.

Cremation – The ashes will be given to the family in an urn or box. If they are to be repatriated, the Crematorium must be advised, as the urn must be sealed appropriately. If you want some ashes to be scattered in France, and some sent back home you can ask for 2 urns, one of which will be sealed. Most cemeteries have areas set aside for the burial of ashes, but you can take them home. They may not be scattered in public areas, roads or rivers. The *Mairie* will record the date and where the ashes are scattered.

As soon as you can make an appointment to see your *Notaire*, who will want to see the following documents, including the will if he or she hasn't already got a copy (although less than 10% of folks in France do have a will):

- Death certificate (to be requested from the town hall of the place of death)
- Details of the deceased person and that of the children
- Photocopy of the identity card (passport for non-French citizens)
- Marriage certificate of the deceased person
- Gifts between spouses
- Gifts to children
- The deceased's bank accounts
- Names and addresses of pension providers
- Title deeds

- Registration document of the deceased's (and spouse's) motor vehicle(s)
- Life insurance contract
- Taxes details - foncière, habitation, income
- Invoice for funeral expenses paid
- The Name of the children with profession, address, telephone and email

Inform all utility companies, pension companies, state pension authorities as soon as you can because if there are any overpayments they will have to be paid back.

Note that British Credit Cards are only in one person's name and therefore that person is the only one responsible for paying it off (or the Estate of). That means that if you are only a named cardholder, that credit card will no longer be available for your use.

ABOUT THE AUTHOR

Jane LeMaux, a British national was born and grew up in Kenya. Jane was mainly educated in the UK and worked in Information Technology in several other countries before retiring to France.

She has therefore faced settling in several countries and knows how difficult that can be even when you think you are speaking the same language, let alone speaking a completely different language. She has used these experiences to pull together the information in this book.

POSTSCRIPT

Whilst writing this book, new suggestions for inclusion popped up most days and there are always points of debate. So, if you feel you'd like to add something spot an error or disagree with something I've written, please don't hesitate to email me on SettlingInFrance@gmail.com.

RECIPE INDEX

Printed in Great Britain
by Amazon

80777438R00129